THE APPLICANT

AN INSIDER'S GUIDE TO THE COLLEGE ADMISSIONS
PROCESS

ISHAN PURI

TABLE OF CONTENTS

Part 1: The Approach

Part 2: Building Passion

Part 3: Along the Journey

Part 4: Academics

Part 5: Showing Personality and Sharing Your Story

Part 6: The Final Stretch

Part 7: Resources

ACKNOWLEDGEMENTS

I would not have been able to write this book without the support of many individuals. Everyone who has supported me indirectly or directly deserves to be co-author because they shape who I am.

In particular, for a variety of reasons I would like to thank: my family immediate and distant for giving me courage, my mentors and teachers who have guided me every step of the way, and all of my peers for shaping my thinking. I would love to write every name down but that would take the entirety of this book plus more. You are all in my heart.

I dedicate this book to the spirit of excellence and genius that exists in all of us.

Thank you.

INTRODUCTION

WHY THIS ADMISSIONS GUIDE?

There are not many college admissions guides — or any actually that I have seen — written by students who have recently gone through the process and who formally think about their experiences and teach about them in classes. This guide I have created after experiencing the actual process very recently and I think that I have a perspective that is very similar to many of my audience members'. I wrote this book because I want to make the process easier and I wanted to share what I learned from the process. I want to share what worked, what did not, and how I approached the process. This guide is written by a student for students, parents, and educators interested in the process and interested in learning more about the student's perspective of the journey.

More importantly, this text follows the mantra of the **Perspective Approach**. Instead of just focusing on how to better write essays, the **Perspective Approach** analyzes why we write essays and why we go through interviews, giving meaning to these activities before diving into them. Then we approach how to do these activities, combining meaning and action. We take this same approach to the college essay writing process, instead of just fixing small grammar and spelling errors here and there. At first this method may seem strained and difficult to accept because we are so used to blindly trying to succeed, but eventually I hope students, parents, and educators see the benefit of understanding "why?" before aimlessly trying to write. The approach requires patience, but aims to build something much harder than getting into college first: it aims to build strong and moral minds and as a byproduct the successful college applicant, the successful job applicant, and the successful applicant for life. Its long term goal is to build a value for education in our youth's mind and a value for excellence. It is more than a how-to or self-help guide.

Thank you for supporting my work. I wrote this work because I feel there are major gaps between admission decisions, conceptions about the process, and students that need to be filled. I make an attempt at filling these gaps by looking at my own recent experiences in the system, my contemporaries' experiences, and the literature I have read. The admissions process is indeed a system that needs to be understood so that you can succeed. Nobody can deny that it is a system. But it is a system that cannot be "beat" — do not believe those texts that promise this in any way. The system can only be understood better. By understanding the way it works, the ideas behind its different aspects, students can become more knowledgeable. The system also has luck involved — if the admissions officer reading your application just happens to "click" with you, you might be in luck. I am very open to students' opinions to the different aspects in my work and I will update future versions with their input. The key is input. I think this work is not a novella or novel — it is a hands-on working guide to the admissions process written with collective wisdom to help those in the process, concerned parents, and students who want to learn more.

INSIGHT INTO THE AMERICAN SYSTEM

I have experience in the American admissions process as that is the process I recently went through. Through my conversations with contemporaries from Australia, South Korea, India, China, and several other nations, I see that the college application process within different nations is indeed unique at each of these locations. For example, in the European admissions system, I know that students must apply within specific schools and for specific subjects. The selection process is significantly harder for some subjects or schools, and the prestige is based on subject/college within universities. This kind of system requires a different set of exams as well (A levels are one set) and I am sure that some other particulars are necessary. Through consulting with my peers across the world, I have been able to use their personal insight in writing chapters dedicated to international students applying to US schools.

MY PERSONAL APPROACH

My refined personal approach plays into this book. My view on the process is interweaved into the aspects I found most important through the nine years that I have been involved in the system consciously. My approach has been to do the best I possibly can and I think that this approach works for all students. Some call it overachieving, others call it unrealistic, and still others label it dreamer. I think it is just hard work.

I understand that all individuals may not be willing to work to their potential. I hope to change that perspective throughout this book, and that is why this book is not a book that claims to have "tricks" or "secrets" — it is however, proven and effective. If you read this book in full, you may see my perspective. For those who do work hard, you will understand what I mean when I espouse my philosophies sometimes.

If you are a senior, I encourage you to read this book in entirety. But if you are really short on time, do not hesitate to skip around. This is not a novel, it is a hands-on guide to the admissions process in which I try to understand the process I went through recently.

THE ADMISSIONS OFFICE PERSPECTIVE

Throughout this work, I try to take the perspective of an applicant and consider the perspective of admissions officers and of the interviewer. I try to imagine what it would be like to be in their shoes and what I would look for. After all, they are just as human as we are. I have consulted with many admissions officers in regards to their views, and have found them to be similar to what I thought they would be. Think about it: they have dedicated several months to reading thousands and thousands of applications to pick the next batch of students for their university. Some of them may have been or are faculty members and some may have even been students at the said university. They want the best for the university and by deciding if you will "fit" or not they are finding what is best for you. You just have to write about yourself. I think they have the even harder job to postulate into the future and to see if you will use the resources available to a maximum and to hypothesize whether you will be happy at their university.

CREATIVITY AND THE SELF

Viewed in entirety, the application process is a process of self-reflection and a time to tell your story. It is a time of understanding for the student. For some, it is very helpful to start tinkering with a personal answer to the big question: what is my role in the world? In the end, I offer advice in this text that I draw from my own experiences and from the experiences of my contemporaries. Perhaps you will take some of these tips, perhaps you will reject some. But my goal is to help you *embrace* the process — understand its aim and its purpose. After you embrace the entire process (including the exams associated) you will do much, much better. You understand *why* you are doing something: **the Perspective Approach**.

The process is a creative one. There are no true guidelines, even for the most quantitative aspects (the SAT/ACT, Subject Tests, GPA). I know people who were accepted to Ivy League schools and similar institutions with sub-2000 SAT scores and some who scored 2400. There is a lot of luck in the matter. All I can *really* recommend to you is to try your best, which you inherently will if you embrace the process. Also, be yourself. They want to know about *you*, not about all the techniques you learned to master the timing on the SAT or how to do minimal work in AP English in order to get an

A. Even the techniques in this book are designed to be guidelines for you. The entire point of these strategies is to help you *show* how you are to admissions officers. It is to facilitate you in telling your story and to understand the system so that you can find every nook and cranny where you can insert a part of your life. Through this process, these methods have the end goal of showing your passion for university, for education, and eventually for life. Your passion will be unique and different from everyone around you—including your identical twin if you have one. You will be you and it should show in your application. That is the objective of the process! To *become* you.

First off, although many students gloat about "achievements" I think they are nothing to gloat about. These kinds of students have not embraced the process but instead mock it. The process includes not only the admissions process. It includes your academic growth, your social growth, and your creative growth. You do not need to tell people that you *enjoy* studying because most people will not understand you and will mock you. Instead, remain quiet. Do you work and be passionate about what you do. That is the best way. But do not reject the process because your friends reject it. Think deep about what you are doing and embrace it because it *feels* right and because it *is* right.

PART 1: THE APPROACH

THE PHILOSOPHY/THE PERSPECTIVE METHOD

The journey to college can be daunting, exciting, and educational simultaneously. We must embrace whatever we chose to do in order to do well. The key to a successful college admissions process is an *embracement* by the student — a recognition of the importance of the process for admission officers and for themselves. This is the one facet that I have noticed in all students who have successfully completed the admissions process. Truly successful college applications — and eventually students and members of the workforce — understand why we go through the tedious processes that life sometimes throws at us. They have been developed for a reason. I will give examples of this perspective:

1. 1ST-8TH GRADES

FOR THE PARENTS (this section is dedicated to the philosophy that parents should adopt during this time. Students, you can skip over this section.)

Many students tend to overlook the importance of their early careers. Parents, at least to my experience, usually see this importance. Why is there a separation in ideas?

Some may say that asking 5th grade students to start planning for their future may be absurd. But that is not what I am suggesting. Instead, parents must inspire their children. I understand this is harder said than done, but let us try to analyze this statement.

Many parents valiantly expose their children to television programs, books, and magazines that promise a "genius" child or "reading at a higher level". Indeed, some of these methods work, but only with constant attention and diligence which busy parents do not have the time for. My parents tried the same with me, and I can remember after the first week this "training" became inconsistent. If, however, parents are able to keep to a daily schedule of these activities, I strongly recommend these readings and viewings. They have been developed for that purpose.

The previous case, in which a parent creates a daily schedule of "doses" of educational material, is highly time-consuming and most likely unpractical. Instead of using time to try this approach, I recommend other tactics.

First, exposing children to different fields — however elementary — can work. I term this the **shotgun approach**. Elementary math, which can be taught through educational toys that can be given to children, is an example. Another is teaching geography by giving realistic, topographic maps that children can play with. Sometimes, children show an affinity for one of these areas, and if they continue to do so as you show them more and more complicated activities in the same realm, this may be their budding interest.

In early elementary school years, exposing children to various extracurricular activities could also uncover or develop a passion. This is a variation on the "shotgun" approach. This approach could entail drama productions, trumpet lessons, or even math competitions.

In addition to this "shotgun" approach, *read* to them, at least four times a week. This is *especially* important for mental growth early on. The next critical step, which many do not take, is to encourage children to *read* themselves:

Reading is the key to developing a clear line of though, critical thinking skills, and writing.

Eventually, I would encourage children to develop mentors—especially at an early age. They tend to naturally do this—for example, Winnie the Pooh may be a mentor. However, I would expose children to mentors who have succeeded in the real world through hard, honest work. These mentors could be baseball players, mathematicians, or explorers. Children will see the commonalities among these individuals and may become inspired.

This exposure could occur through the classroom but I would encourage parents to actively develop mentors through readings, through extracurricular activities, and through conversation.

At this stage, parents can do a few things to *inspire* and *further* development:

1. **Shotgun Effect**
    a. Exposure Through Academia
        i. Educational "curriculums"= books that further reading levels, television series that further development

   1. Only pursue if this can be done consistently and on a daily, structured schedule

  ii. Educational "toys"= topographic maps, globes, puzzles…

 b. Exposure Through Extracurricular Activities

  i. Drama Plays

  ii. Mathematic/Science Competitions

  iii. Music/Singing Lessons

2. Reading—CRITICAL—Regardless of the results of the Shotgun Effect, reading should be enforced initially then should come naturally

 a. Parents read to young scholars

  i. "Indirect inspiration"—this reading could focus on discoveries, explorers, or innovation and resulting success through hard work

  ii. "Indirect Shotgunning"—this reading could focus **instead** on various academic fields

 b. **Students read themselves**

  i. This is perhaps the most important of all the advice I have given regarding inspiration. Getting students to read will help them discover what they love or develop a sprouting passion.

The more children read, the more they learn and the better they are able to communicate through the word. The readings do not have to initially be sophisticated — they just have to be *numerous*. It could be reading *Dr. Seuss* many times over, but reading is the key.

One of the things I regret is not having develop a specific passion early on. I do remember recalling the importance of academics at an early age — it was *self-realization* heavily facilitated by my parents and my surroundings. If I could change one aspect of my high school career it would be developing a passion early on, say in 7th or 8th grade, and continuing to work on that. Still, I have no regrets and am grateful for realizing the importance of specialization at an early age.

The outline is fairly vague in regards to specific ages that students should start developing passions because this process will be different for every student and child. While you try to consciously promote learning and specialization, try and let it flow *naturally*. Yes, this is counter-intuitive and illogical, but I believe this is the way that many things are in life. Have the end-goal in mind, and perhaps develop checkpoints (by 8th grade have developed a specialty) but do not overpower the child. It is *their* life. If there is one thing I am most grateful for, it is for the freedom of choice that my parents gave me. This freedom is the most important aspect of the process.

The Shotgun Effect

Educational "Toys"

Puzzles

Maps

Games

Building Passion

Reading

Establish a structured reading schedule

"Facilitated reading"

Activities

Plays

Competitions

Family Time

The essence of these activities is to build passion.
Facilitated reading is reading your own material, whether
it be a newspaper or magazine, physically with your child
while they read something on their own in order to
encourage them to read. I recommend doing this reading
at least once a week for 30 minutes at a time, a specific day
and time, perhaps Saturday at 8PM.

Parents! Do not get caught up in the details and competition!

Parents

Students

Focus on results

Focus on race

Focus on winning awards rather than the process

Stressed to succeed

Pressured to do without knowing why

Less sucess

2. 9TH AND 10TH GRADES

The student has had time to explore and the opportunity to explore many different areas through in-class activities, extracurricular ventures, and parental support. In my honest opinion, at this point the student should try and start focusing in on a **niche** that they can specialize in. Ideally, this should begin at the start of 9th grade, but exploration in 9th grade is perfectly fine as well. That is what I did. There are two reasons for this **niche** approach:

1. By this time, the student has dabbled in a few areas. It is time to focus in and see if our capability matches our interest. Even if it does not at this stage, developing our passion *will* develop our capabilities. Earlier is always better.
   a. We can *all* develop each talent endlessly. Hopefully, parents have inspired them to pursue education for the number of benefits it brings. Initially, it is understandable if our defiant 2nd grader do not want to "do anything". Initial pushing is usually necessary. But after a certain stage, the student realizes why their parents are pushing them. At this point, students *fully* engage themselves in whatever activities they do. In this way, they can get a fuller *flavor* of the various fields they could pursue. It is entirely possible that this realization

stage comes during 5th grade, 7th grade, or even 11th grade. At some point, I believe most students realize this. I have some friends in college who are realizing why their parents pushed them. This is really not a problem. Let me repeat for the worried parents out there: realizing later is always better than never, and most people realize at some point. The purpose of my previous attempts where to catalyze this process, which could make the entire exercise of education easier and smoother for both student and parent. Ultimately, the student really determines what kind of route they are going to take. The parents' job is the *inspire* instead of *push*. Easier said than done, I know, but I have outlined a few ways in the previous sections.

2. In the world, individuals must specialize in a particular field. Although most times our interest change from high school, some students develop an organic passion that they follow throughout their lives. Why not develop it earlier and get a head start?

FOR THE PARENTS

They are many ways parents can still be involved in the process of development. First, realize that students need a little more freedom now. They are starting to develop their own identities and their own ideas about things. They need some room for thought.

Second, being loving and caring is always helpful. As student start to experience hard material, AP or honors classes, the workload becomes more. Parents can easy students into this by loving them and making sure they eat on time every day. Make sure you are not texting them every day though.

Third, this may not be necessary if the student is very motivated already, is to search for extracurricular activities that could light an interest or augment an existing one.

FOR THE STUDENTS

We are in high school now. Now you have responsibility and you must organize your time. **Time management** becomes important now, especially if you are ambitious and want to pursue significant extracurricular activities and develop socially, culturally, and intellectually.

THE FRESHMAN YEAR MYTH:

Some upperclassmen and college students will tell you that freshman year does not matter. Let me tell you: IT DOES. Every single year matters because it is time that you *could* be practicing your time management skills, honing your interests, and developing social ties to the community, to friends, and to like-minded students around the world. At the same time, just try your best. Half of the battle is knowing that every year counts. Then you will start working harder because YOU are motivated to work.

At this point, you should begin to feel comfortable managing your own work, this includes studying for exams, quizzes, and homework. Initially, specifically the first few months of 9th grade, should be a transition for you. It was definitely difficult for me. But I managed and got used to it. The keys are **time management**, **prioritization**, and **focus**. Let me give you examples of each so you know exactly what I mean.

Time management can mean different things to different people.

1. **Time-Oriented Management:**
   a. For me, it was starting to do homework every day at 5 PM. I would take a 30 minute eating break when I came back from school, then a 30 minute nap. Then I would get up and start studying at 5 PM. I was not so stringent to define which subjects I would study at what time, I just did what I thought I could do at that time but made sure everything was finished. If I finished my homework early, I would just start reviewing for next week's exam, for instance. As I began to get involved in various clubs and extracurricular activities, this management became critical. Soon, my Saturdays were spent researching at UCLA and so I had to work harder during the weekdays.
   b. This strategy emphasizes regularity of study time, place of study, and how

studying is done. I find that most people benefit from this strategy.

2. **Task-Oriented Management:**

   a. This type of management is for a select group of people in my opinion. In this style, regularity is not necessary to the completion of tasks. Instead, they focus on the task and can disregard time, place, or noise level. For example, I had a few friends in high school who came straight home from school and began studying. Sometimes, they would take a break but often they would not. They finished their work at the same pace that I did, but just in a little more "random" fashion. They could work on the couch with the TV on or in their room, but they still managed to complete the work because they focused on the task.

   b. I also notice however, that effective task-oriented management turns into time-oriented management if the tasks are completed effectively. Some of my core group of friends and scholars in high school would complete tasks in a specific order every day unknowingly.

For most people, I recommend **time-oriented management**, because I have seen that it works with a majority of students.

Prioritization:

Prioritization is one of the THE most important skills that successful students gain in late primary school and early high school stages. We have the opportunity *what* to involve ourselves in and so we must chose. As a freshman in high school, I joined 21 clubs during Club Week. Within two weeks, this number dwindled to 3. I feel that this is a natural process, as long as we eventually *chose* which organizations to involve ourselves in. Even in college, I joined about 6 organizations. One quarter into college, I have *chosen* 3 to stay involved in.

I term this the **tunneling process**. We are presented with a world of options, and soon we must *tunnel* our choices to a few. These activities should all revolved around a central theme, as I should describe later.

Since middle school, I feel like I have had a hierarchy that has done me well. It is a priority scheme:

1. Health
2. Academics (Grades, SAT/ACT)
3. Extracurricular Activities
4. Friends/Networking

This is usually true, although sometimes my parents question if health is below academics. This is not to say that I have few friends either! I do not study all the time! No, instead I spend the most *valuable* hours of the day on activities ranked higher. If I have free time, say a Friday afternoon, I will surely relax with friends. Just make sure that your time allotment is relative to these categories — make sure most of your time is spent on academics and on developing that **niche**. One way to check yourself is to write down in your journal what you did each day and how much time you spent on it. Make sure it adds up to 24 hours so you are realistic with yourself.

By developing a schedule for each day's activities, you are inherently also prioritizing. This is one of the reason I feel that success is exponential: the factors leading to it are linked!

Focus

Perhaps the most important and the broadest of all the skills we develop in high school is **focus**. I think that **focus** is key because it is a lifelong skill that we constantly use in any task. My definition of **focus**:

Focus (n) : The ability to concentrate on a particular task without any distractions for the time it takes to complete that task in entirety and with highest quality.

Basically, it is the ability to isolate yourself and work until completion on a task without worrying about anything else, including time. This is where I have a qualm with many teaching styles. Some styles and training methods emphasize *time* as a direct relation to *quality*. This is indeed not so.

An Introduction to Student A and B

Throughout this book, we will occasionally use Student A and B to describe two approaches to different tasks, whether it be focusing or writing college admissions essays. Student A is a student who is not aware and has not developed a meaning for education for himself/herself. Student B is a student who has developed meaning for learning in his/her life and has an internal drive and motivation.

Student A comes home from school. He eats for 30 minutes and then relaxes for 30 minutes. He goes to his room to study at 5 PM. He does not leave but comes down for dinner at 8 PM. Whether he did work or was on Facebook during that time is ultimately *his choice* and *his responsibility*. Having spent three hours on that math assignment, while chatting on iChat, AIM, and Facebook at the same time does not entail that he completed his assignment.

Student B, on the other hand, went to his room, checked Facebook for 5 minutes and then closed it and shut off his phone. He worked on his math set for one hour and finished it. He also was able to check it once over. By dinner time, he has finished his math, English, and history homework. He now has about 4 hours to work on studying for future exams, doing extracurricular activities, or reading or writing. He constantly is improving himself and is in what I call **constant focus**. This state is achieved when we become so comfortable with focus that we can shift between activities and also maintain focus. However, even when we have reached this stage, a break every one hour or one and a half hours can be beneficial to re-sharpening focus.

Focus is beneficial for so many things. There are a few ways I have found that help me sharpen my focusing skills consciously besides removing all distractions and working on a single activity until completion:

1. Meditation. Although this may sound odd, meditation has definitely helped me maintain **focus** and gain **constant focus**. Meditation can be spiritual but can also be non-spiritual. For example, meditation for me is sometimes sitting outside focusing on a single petal of a flower for as long as can, disregarding everything around me. This task is much harder said than done, try it. Try focusing on something without any distractions for five minutes. Set a timer then try and forget everything except that one object. Another activity is to try and think about *nothing*. I have found this to be one of the hardest challenges. Close your eyes and try this now.

2. Incremental Simulations. These simulations can be of anything. To start, try focusing on staying on Facebook without doing anything else for five minutes. That was easy, right? Now try writing a Word document for five minutes. A little more difficult, I am sure. Now move to your work. Repeat this process until you have completely mastered each step. I suggest doing these simulations in your free time, however, as they take time.

11TH AND 12TH GRADES

Now you should have thoroughly developed your skills in **time management**, **prioritization**, and **focus**. If you are a junior or senior reading this book, skim over the past few chapters to get an idea of what skills you will need for college studies and for jobs. In any case, you can indeed still develop these skills! That is the beauty of the process. We are still so young. It will require more intense training however. For example, you may have to practice mediation for 30 minutes a day in order to gain the focus necessary to do very well in academics and anything you put your mind to. In any case, if you are a junior or senior and are reading this, you have developed these three skills to some extent, otherwise you would not be in 11th or 12th grade.

WHY GO TO COLLEGE?

Before starting your essays, first consider why you are going to college or why you want your child to go to college. What is the reason? This is *the most important step in the admissions process*. Once you find that personal reason, the process becomes less stressful and more successful.

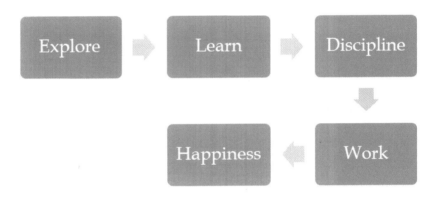

This path is often the one that people take and what parents hope that students take. Learn, discipline, and work are what we usually consider the results of college.

How NOT to approach the admissions process or life

College and life is NOT a linear path. Money is not happiness. College does NOT always lead to work and happiness. When people finding <u>meaning</u> in what they do, whether it is studying in college or in their job, then they find happiness.

Try to find why you are going to college, and if the only reason is to get a job, that reason is not good enough. Colleges will see that you are a **linear applicant** with only one motive: a job. They want someone who will take full advantage of their resources, someone who understands that college is more than just a pathway to jobs.

Academics is a critical part of why we go to college. It forms the base of who we are and forms society. Colleges are what keep academics alive, and the admissions process is a gateway to that base of academics, the college. The successful college applicant will have strong academics and be able to focus on passion/activities, and eventually vision. The hope is that these individuals will enter the college and refine their vision, who they want to be and how they want to change the world, through their activities and their perspectives. That is why academics is so stressed in the admissions process and in colleges. Below is the **vision pyramid**, showing that academics, more generally, ideas, form the base of who we are and what we do.

"THE GAME"

The application process is a genuine storytelling process that the applicant has with an admissions office team of experienced individuals. It is not a repeatable, "winnable" game, although it is a process with rules and plenty of myths.

Many counselors, "guidebooks", and even some test preparation books call the admissions process a "game" that can be mastered or conquered. Although there are definitely aspects of the process that seem to have rules and guidelines and suggested paths, it is not a game in that the same algorithm can be repeated over and over for different students from different locations with different backgrounds. But it definitely has rules and unfortunately there are many misconceptions about the process that make people focus on the wrong elements and miss the important elements. One of the purposes of this book it to try and clear some of those misconceptions and stress which parts of the process are important—also delineating how we reach the conclusion about which parts are important and which are not so important.

First, there are certain "recommended" features of the process that *should* be done. Doing them does not guarantee admission but can definitely help: such as the TOEFL exam for international students applying to US schools. Another "recommended" feature for some schools are the number of SAT subject tests to send in. If you have high scores on three SAT subject tests and the school requires two but would recommend three, definitely send the three. The question becomes vaguer if your third score is not so strong—it then comes done to personal judgment. But remember that there are other students submitting three and demonstrating excellence in three subjects whereas you are doing so only in two. That being said, some students go overboard on the SAT subject test category and take seven or eight tests, trying to demonstrate excellence in even more subjects. Do not be one of "those" students. There are other equally, and maybe more, important aspects of the process such as the interview and the essay.

After following the academic rules, such as taking the necessary SAT/ACT, SAT subject tests, AP/IB tests, the key comes down to time management and vision. These two elements will shape how successful you are in your essays, your interview, and your extracurricular activities. They are also critical in developing your theme — this must be done consciously after all! Admissions officers know the life of the student — almost all of them were at one point in your shoes! They know that you need time management skills to accomplish state or nationally-recognized extracurricular activities and they value your success in the extracurricular field for the *values* and *character* they show rather than the actual accomplishment, although it shows where you have placed your efforts and maybe your aptitude.

This book focuses on helping you with time management, **focus**, and vision with the philosophical aspects of this book. The other aspects are there to help you develop your skills at working the parts of the system that can be worked or trained for, such as examinations. There is definitely a method to the madness, and the goal is to help you find your personal method that will result in you conveying yourself accurately and in the strongest light possible to the admissions officers.

AWARENESS

In life and very poignantly demonstrated in this college admissions process just knowing about an event, a competition, and when and where it is occurring is valuable. Often this awareness is what separates those who develop complete portfolios with a well-rounded theme and great academics as well.

Many students are brilliant in studies but are unaware of the possibilities and the importance of extracurricular activities. This phenomenon is especially true for international students applying into the United States. Some students even have an idea about the time and commitment it takes to form a theme, develop a **"big thing"**, and represent yourself accurately during the interview process but do feel it was important or necessary. Half of awareness is knowing when and where different activities are, especially extracurricular activities, and the other half is understanding the importance of these activities in the whole process.

This awareness is key in extracurricular activities. It is especially key in knowing when and where competitions are (say for science fairs), how prestigious and difficult it is

to win these, and how to enter. All of these elements, or most of them, can be learned from Internet websites like

College Discussion. I spent hours and hours on these kinds of websites searching for competitions and then performing a Google search on the competitions I found. You can make yourself aware by reading newspapers, reading blogs, and performing Google searches. It is very time-intensive but if you make yourself alert it becomes easier over time and almost second nature. If you do not think you can do this or do not think you have the time, then it is worthwhile to get a counselor or use your school counselor to increase your awareness. In any case, I often find that there is a lack in understanding the true importance (the second aspect of awareness) of some activities: sometimes some activities are overvalued (like scoring very high on 8 SAT subject tests and devoting too much time to that) while other are undervalued (like developing the self in personal ways, with friends and with teachers).

Make sure to stay aware. If there is one factor that has differentiated "successful" college applicants from ones that are not as successful, it is this factor. Also, in the long-term, I have noticed that individuals who are aware tend to be more successful in life in general: they know what is happening and how certain situations work from previous experiences of others. Keep your eyes open for opportunities, go for them, and be unafraid of failure. For every one of my successes, I had ten failures. But people only remember the successes.

Here are some ways to become aware:

1. Join student school clubs that interest you

      a. Interacting with students that have similar passions will help surface new competitions or events in your specific interest.
2. Read CollegeDiscussion and similar boards
3. Read the newspaper, searching for scholarships or newsworthy competitions
4. Google competitions or activities in your interest
5. Look at university websites in specific pages that interest you
      a. If you are interested in research, look at what is being done by faculty or by student groups interested in research
      b. If you are interested in sports, read what college student groups are doing

Try to create as many channels of knowledge as you can, and you will eventually find activities and competitions that you enjoy.

PART 2: BUILDING PASSION

THE TIMELINE

Regardless of where you are in the process, there are two things you should start doing:

1. Read for 30 minutes at least once a week. Set a time every week and read. Switch between books that you enjoy or nonfiction.
    a. Students in high school should read New York Times or LA Times every day, at least the front page. This only takes a few minutes. Raising your awareness makes you more knowledgeable and gives you a topic to discuss during interviews and maybe a common interest.
    b. Some essays ask you about your favorite book *outside* of class. Developing your interest in reading will allow you to answer this question.
2. Write for 10 minutes at least once a week. This writing time should be directly after reading, in case you cannot **free write** you can summarize what you read. This summary back up is only meant for the first times you write, because writing about yourself can be hard initially.

When should I begin the actual admissions process and start working on essays? This is one of the common questions from students who have time to spare. This is up to you, but there is a general frame of time that you should keep in mind that I have found effective. The Perspective Approach is a long term approach that I have developed, which essentially says start as soon as possible, but in regards to admissions essays and the Common Application, I have detailed a timeline below.

During the first few days of summer after 11th grade, begin to investigate superficially colleges. This means looking at them, where they are, and their websites. If you live nearby a university you might consider attending, visit it now. Just start researching casually universities, their various affiliations, and try to get a feel for the culture of various institutions. During this time, also start talking to friends and contemporaries at some of the institutions. Ask them about their honest opinions about classes, student life, and about anything else that you find interesting about their particular university.

The Common Application is released mid-summer This is when you should start seriously working on your applications. College applications will be on your mind before this point, perhaps at the end of 11th grade. But now you should start adding universities to your list of schools to apply to. Read School-Centric Approach for a more detailed approach of what you should be doing right now. Start making the list of schools you are thinking, even *vaguely*, about applying to. You can always narrow this list down, but you want to start with a broad range of schools that could fit any one of your passions or nascent interests. You should start adding these schools to the Common Application site or to the individual sites that some schools have. Peruse over the questions in the application and pay particular attention to the supplement. Often, the questions universities ask are different and reflect some aspect of that university (see **structured prompt**).

Now your school has started and you have been researching casually for about one and a half months various schools and their personalities. You should have a whittled down, polished list of schools you are applying to, and have started early drafts of your essays, especially your main Common Application essays. Make sure that they are not in any specific order of preference! Please read the end of the chapter "Dream School Predicament" for more on why you should not rank your schools, even by ranges.

By early September, you should have your finalized list and should be starting to work on your essays. Start thinking about what you want to convey and what you think your **theme** is. With this much time, you have space to think and to ponder. This **thinking period** will result in more sophisticated essays that will set you apart. Start with the processes written about in the several chapters about the essays in this text. Either start outlining your essays or start writing them in full.

Within the month of September, create, edit, and finalize your resume, either from your **resume-builder** or from previous versions of your resume. You should be writing your essays from now until either the early action/early decision deadlines for your schools or until early December for regular decision. You should also work on developing your **theme** and your **one-sentence** through your writing (see the chapter "Activity-Building"). From September to the end of December, your focus will be on writing. For more on specifics, please see Part 5: Showing Personality and Sharing Your Story.

By the end of September, plan for any major activities that you plan to do within your extracurricular activities. Also, plan for major competitions that take place in January or beyond, in the case of a waitlist result, this planning will pay great dividends. Planning now will save you time and will allow you to manage the interview process (which takes place in January mostly) with your extracurricular activities.

Throughout, be working on your essays and get as much feedback as you can. Some suggest that having a limited number of people review your application is better. The logic behind this is you do not want to many perspectives going into your essay. Keep your own voice, but also take the opinions of others into consideration — they are reading your essays from an outsider perspective and might read something differently than you do. Also, make sure that you are working hard on your classes as well — first semester grades are critical for waitlisted students and for applying students in general.

THE NICHE

Now you must know or develop your **niche**. This is the where you fall in the college admissions process, where you think you can be "categorized". There are a few well-known niches, but also remember that there are others. Never box yourself in, ever:

1. Athlete
   a. You are being recruited for your athletic abilities and also strong academics, you are usually seriously recruited starting in 11th grade — the key here is performance on the state or national level, if possible. I have talked about the recruitment process with many athletes, and the beginning of contact with colleges varies. Some reached out themselves early on, in sophomore year, and others were contacted in the senior year of high school.
2. Academic
   a. You are being chosen for your academic abilities and for your intellectual vitality — the key here is passion for knowledge and discipline
3. Legacy
   a. You are being chosen for a combination of factors, perhaps your academic abilities solely, but people label you a "legacy" because your family has a strong affiliation with a particular school. Although the blanket title of "legacy" may overshadow

your true academic capabilities and such, it can be an advantage at some institutions.

There are also a few factors to consider when choosing your niche:

1. Ethnicity
   a. Unfortunately, ethnicity still does play a role in college admissions. Students have more choice of whether or not to list ethnicity, if you identify strongly with your ethnic background mark that otherwise you can choose not to answer the questions marked in the grey box on the Common Application.
2. Geographic Location
   a. Some claim that schools also look at where you are from, because location can shape how you think, and colleges want diversity in thought processes. Although you cannot change this aspect of your application, you can be aware that it may influence how admissions look at you.

THE ESSAYS

Student A and Student B have just seen the Common Application and the various supplements provided by schools. It is mid-July. Students A and B will be examples throughout the book.

Student A: Ugh! These college essays are *utterly* pointless! They are so pointless that I will just leave them for the last week of December or the beginning of January. I just want to relax with friends and spend my last few months with them.

Student B: Wow! This is really a lot of writing. However, this is what I have been working towards for a long time. I want to prove to the colleges that I am the one for them. What is a better way than to write to them? This is an *opportunity* not a burden. Perhaps I will set up a specific time each weekend to work. I am ready.

As we can see, realistically both students see the amount of work that college essays can be.

Student A seems to be similar to many college applicants, viewing the process from the start as a *burden*. Student B views

it instead as an *opportunity*.

This initial outlook on the process will help you infinitely. Not only will your essays likely be stronger, but during interviews you are more likely to shine through because of your enthusiasm and understanding of the process.

The first step is really that simple, yet that complicated.

Tell yourself:

I *love* this process.

It sounds cheesy, but it works. You will eventually grow to accept it, at least.

A Further Analysis of Student B (The Successful Applicant):

The successful applicant realizes that the process is necessary and is not only about writing superficial essays. These essays are an *opportunity* for admissions officers to see how students *think* and also a tool for self-exploration. Why do you want an education? Who are you? Great essays probe students to think about these things and come to an initial answer. That is why this book focuses on aspects like "building passion" and "showing yourself". Of course, our answers to these questions do not have to be static. They can change and probably should as we experience more and more of life. Students realize that these essays have two goals, one pragmatic and the other relatively lofty:

1. Essays give an insight into the way students think. College admissions officers craft a student body around different perspectives that will hopefully create a cohesive, enriching, and enjoyable environment. You should try to pose yourself as someone else, but realize that they are looking to "define" you, or at least most of you, through your essays (especially), your grades, your test scores, and your interview.

2. Student B takes the essay seriously. For him/her, one essay prompt along the road hits home. Who *am* I? What do I see myself as in the future and how am I different from everyone else? I truly believe everyone is unique in some aspect — bringing this out in your application, and believing it, can be greatly beneficial.

The philosophy of the successful applicant is the first step towards a successful admissions process and a successful person, although going to a great college is not always correlated to being a great person. The aim of this book is to make great, honest people, and through that successful applicants, and that is why it is different than many, if not all, "admissions books" on the market, and the most effective. Understanding this process will help you understand other processes in the future, whether they be the Krebs Cycle or how the company you intern at operates. The Perspective Approach applies to all aspects of life.

ACTIVITY-BUILDING

Another important aspect, closely tied to your resume, is activity-building. Throughout your high school career, choose activities that can be grouped together logically and that focus on your **theme**. Your **theme** is an abstract idea that you will focus your essays on. I believe that through your activities you can concretely demonstrate your theme and other quality traits that are important in showing Personality and Drive, Applicant Aspect 4.

So how do you choose your activities? I gave a backbone outline in the previous chapter about having some in-school and out-of-school activities. That is the general principle. But what about the specifics, how many activities should I engage in and of what level of participation should I engage in.

The first thing to consider is that academics come before your **theme** and your activities. If you are engaged in too many activities and you must start studying so much less that your grades start to fall, then you should cut back on your activities. On the other hand, you do not want to find yourself playing Xbox or visiting friends every week. This means that you have too much free time. It is a careful balance that you will realize eventually if you try.

To accurately develop your activities, you first need to figure out your **theme**. Without this, it is not possible to gauge which activities to join. Remember your **theme** is based on a passion, so the activities will flow naturally. It is an organic process and every student can do it, it is about sitting down and actually thinking and getting somewhere that many students do not do.

The earlier you develop your **theme**, the more time you have to choose your activities and develop yourself within those activities (gaining experiences that you may use in your essays, gain experience, and possible leadership). For me, I started developing my **theme** in 9th grade. I took the shotgun approach to joining clubs, so I had joined too many organizations. Quickly the number whittled down. I would say that by the end of 10th grade you should have a solid list of activities that you are involved in—these are significantly different than competitions in that they require constant attention and involvement.

There is always the balance between being specific and being flexible in your activities. If you have more time and are starting activity-building earlier, you will be able to be more flexible. If you are an 11th grader, you will need to focus your activities on fewer passions. If you have to choose one, always go with specific. Eventually you have to become specific for your **theme**.

SO WHAT DO I ACTUALLY JOIN?

Flexibility ↑

Do many activities and get a flavor for them (early on)

Show that you can do so much

Choose one topic and be totally focused on it (often for the sake of admissions only)

Show your focus and drive

Specificity ↓

I think that students should join organizations that they really want to be in. There are usually many organizations at schools, in particular, clubs, that students should join. Join the school clubs, or even better, create clubs at your school that revolve around your **theme**. I would say that you should join between 1-3 clubs at your school. I personally would stay on the lower side of this scale because I realized that if you want to run a club correctly, even a school club, you need a lot of time and attention. Focus on fewer clubs and become specialized in these clubs. With this approach, you can show passion to those who are currently running the club and get elected to positions in sophomore, junior, or senior year. I would say that leadership, a character aspect that contributes to Applicant Aspect 4 (Personality and Drive) is NECESSARY for admissions to all colleges. Leadership is often shown through involvement in school clubs (President, Vice President and so forth). If you can found a club, that is even better, especially if it becomes significant. Think about what this shows: commitment to a task, leadership, and vision. It seems that almost every applicant to top schools has founded some sort of organization.

After getting involved in a few school clubs (very few) and striving to become leaders of these, I would say that out-of-school involvement is next. *The level of your out-of-school activities often determines the strength of your theme and many times admissions to colleges, especially top colleges.* The key here is the "level" of your activities. This level is determined by the scale of your activities, which I categorize into three areas:

1. Local—This organization operates within the city or between cities. There are numerous organizations throughout the globe that operate

like this, and so your involvement here must be coupled with a leadership position and perhaps an individual change you made in order to be somewhat significant. Make sure, again, that you join an appropriate organization outside of school that fits with your **theme**.

2. State — This is the next level of the organization. These are recognized entities — such as interning for the state governor — that are respected. Getting involved at the state level in *anything* that is repeated (an activity) is the first differentiating factor between admissions to top 15 and top 30 colleges, in my opinion. This is estimation, but in my experiences and with the experiences with my friends, this is what I have found. State or nationwide organization that have local branches (such as Kiwanis club) do not count — they are still considered local organizations.

3. National — Often activities do not reach this level. If they do, it is by your individual effort and will usually be your **"big thing"**. Initiative, drive, vision, and passion will bring an organization to this level.

4. International — Very, very few organizations reach this level. Often at the national and international level activities become morphed into competitions.

These out-of-school activities can be anything from research to founding a business. It is really up to you. Because of this freedom, many times students do not even attempt to create an activity for themselves or get involved. Make sure that your activity, especially your out-of-school activity, has **scope**. This means that it can be scaled upwards and can reach at least the state level. In my opinion, once you start having activities at the state level, you start to differentiate yourself significantly from the rest of the applicant pool. I look for this particularly in students applying to top schools.

These out-of-school activities are important because they inherently show initiative. You go out and search for these activities, chose which one fits your passion, and then do it fully. If you can gain a leadership position in any of these, it is even better because now you show vision and leadership. In my opinion, you should try and gain a leadership position in every one of your activities if possible. This is a reoccurring **thread** that admissions officers can see. The more **threads** that you have, the more sophistication and thought was put into your application and the more appreciation and **"hits"** you can get from admissions officers. All it takes is one **"hit"** — one thing that clicks between you and an admissions officer.

Now there is a significant difference between activities and competitions. Activities are things that you are constantly involved in, such as clubs, organizations, or even school plays. Competitions are singular events that give you the possibility of an award or honor. Both are necessary for a strong base.

The advantage of competitions is that they can scale on the national or international level. However, these kinds of competitions often require dedication to a particular field and a significant work, whether it be an essay, a scientific paper, or an art piece. They really require persistence, vision, and skill. For this reason, admissions officers weigh them heavily. In many of my contemporaries who were successful at these large competitions and in my own experience, an activity usually leads to a successful application to these competitions. For example, I did linguistics research every Saturday at UCLA. I also spent most of my Sundays reviewing what we spoke about and working on the paper. After one year of this, I had a concrete paper, which I entered into the California State Science Fair. I was honored to win 1st place in 11th grade. The Fair was a competition at the state scale, whereas my research was activity. One grew into the other. I could not have entered the Fair without the work I put in to my activity. If you can develop a similar cohesiveness between your activities and your competitions, you will be very strong. Interrelated activities and competitions mean that your work can be used in two places at once. Working hard is one thing, working smart is another entirely.

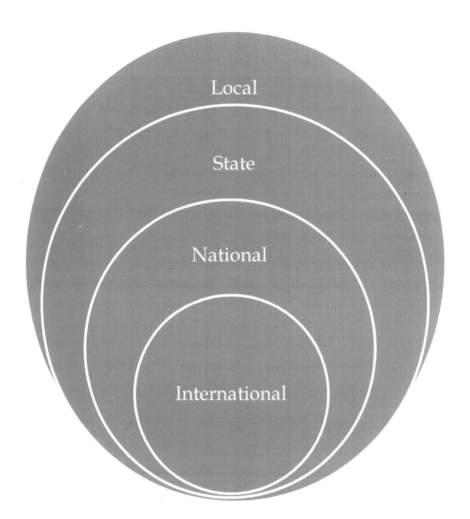

Availability and Impact of Extracurricular Activities

There are many local competitions, fewer statewide, fewer nationwide, and even fewer that are international. Often, you must advance from local to state, and the smaller the number of competitions, the more recognized and the more impact they can have.

There are a few exercises that I have students do when thinking about which activities to join to build out a more complete theme. The **activity document** lists current activities under the heading of local, regional, state, and sometimes national. In parenthesis are listed activities that can be done in the future. Activities are highlighted by color to show continuity among the different scopes (local, regional, state). Hopefully, there is a solid color that links the different scopes, because then a student has shown interest at many levels. If not, then we work to create that thread. Here is an example:

Another exercise I have students do is complete an

Local
Psych Club
(Education Club)--First meeting by end of February
CFY Club --Wednesday

Regional
CFY

State
(Start an international, education-focused, computer nonprofit)---Maybe China? 501(c)(3) filings etc.

arts document. In this, student list the books they enjoy the most or have been reading during their 30 minutes required every week. It could also include specific articles from blogs, movies, or anything related to the arts. This document comes in handy when students are writing about themselves in the college admissions essay.

Common Activities:

Debate	Science Fair	Arts
• School Debate Team • Local Competitions	• Competitions • Published papers with professors	• Poetry • Essay contests in history, art, science, mathematics

BUILDING A THEME

Building a theme is arguably the most important part of your application, in my opinion. It allows you to tell a story. Developing a central, focused theme is one of the *most effective* ways to communicate yourself accurately, succinctly, and poignantly to the admissions officers.

The theme can be *anything*. It can be the passion you have for your family even. It can be your love of anime. Contrary to popular belief, it does not have to be big competitions or events, although it can be. Your theme merely shows dedication to a particular area of life (whether it be artistic, academic, or anything else) and **focus**.

Ideally, the exercises I have denoted in the previous chapters have helped identify *some* vague area in which either you are good at or think you can become good at. I personally came upon my theme in the summer after 10th grade. With hindsight, this is too late. But as always, late is better than never. If you are in any grade up to 12th, you still have ample time to develop your theme. I firmly believe this notion. But as you have less and less time, you have to work has to be more concentrated in order to have a well-defined and believable resume and theme.

Here comes the beautiful part of the developing a theme: it is an entirely *creative, individualistic* experience. It can be anything. But it must be *something*. Most applicants might realize the need for a theme, but they really do not push themselves to develop one. **Effort** becomes essential, especially in this stage of your career (early high school).

How do you build a theme? First, one must explore possible passions and interests. This exploration is what I have been encouraging in the past few chapters. Ideally, this exploration should be done during elementary up through the end of 9th grade. The early that you hone in, the more time you have to develop your interest. However, even if you start in 11th grade, you can *still* develop a solid theme but the work becomes compressed because the time is less.

After exploration, chose a topic. I have developed a method to test if a theme is viable in the process.

First, chose an area that you are interested in. Explore the "extracurricular" — by this I mean anything "outside of class" — opportunities that relate to your specific field of interest.

For example:

Sciences:

Explore the research opportunities that relate to your field.

1. Do these opportunities require laboratory access? How much time are you willing to commit and do you like the lifestyle of the researcher?

Explore the policy aspects or social aspects of science

1. Do you have interest in the social aspects of science? Perhaps consider internships in Washington relating to policy or research in sociology/psychology or related fields.

Humanities

1. Consider competitions that you could enter. These could be trivia related to your field of interest—say history. Usually these competitions entail broader fields such as the history instead of Colonial American History—which may be your **specificity hook**.
2. Consider writing competitions. These competitions can get quite competitive and some will require weeks of preparation in terms of research and pre-writing.

Athletics:

1. First, as most will say, will be consider entering athletic competitions and entering this niche.
2. Academic studies of athletics: There are plenty of academic fields, such as sports medicine, that relate medicine, athletics, training, and biology. Consider field research or research in the laboratory.

There are different **areas of concentration** that these themes can fall in:

1. Academic
   a. Lab Research
   b. Field Research

      c. College-affiliated activities

2. Athletic

      a. Sports Competitions

3. Community

      a. Community Service—related to your theme

          i. Spreading awareness of the importance of dental hygiene in India

      b. Peer Health

      c. Sociological or related field work

After deciding on your **area of concentration** and your approach you must get to the practical aspect.

Research: I had no research connections (for example, my father is not the owner of a physics laboratory or part of an organization that does field research). To be honest, I think that this was an *opportunity* that made me stronger and want me to do research even more.

For me, academic research was my **area of concentration**. In January of my sophomore year I began contacting professors around the nation asking if I could do summer research with them (in particular, in linguistics). More than half did not respond. Let us be realistic. Most professors get hundreds of emails every day and sometimes they just skip over yours. Other times, they just do not have the time to respond. However, after about 4 months of searching, a professor at UCLA, which was relatively close, said he would be interested in being my mentor. We ended up working together for 3 years. It was one of the most enriching experiences of my life. The entire process — including finding my mentor — was truly meaning to me.

In a similar way, you can approach the different **areas of concentration**. The key is initiation. I took the initiative to email professors and go around the system of having to be in college in order to do research. Find a way. I realize that this is really vague and clichéd, but the process of focusing in particularly on your extracurricular is an organic and individual process — which as I said — is both beautiful but frustrating at times.

Here is a backbone that I have seen done before, not meaning that you need to do all of these to be successful:

1. Create or join school clubs that relate to your theme
   a. Examples: Robotics Club, Gavel Club
2. Create or join out-of-school organizations (usually citywide or sometimes statewide) that relate to your theme
   a. Examples: Science service clubs, Debate Tournaments, Tennis Tournaments, Mock Trial Tournaments
3. Not absolutely critical, but can bel important: do something that you *initiate* related to your theme
   a. Examples: self-initiated research, founding of a nonprofit, starting your own company

> ## COMMUNITY SERVICE MYTH
>
> There is a general misconception among parents, students, and some educators that students need to do community service. Sometimes, this idea is extended that the area of community service does not matter — as long as the student does community service this can be "checked off" the necessary checklist of activities.
>
> While I agree that community service is critical and should be in any application, I think that the service should be oriented towards your theme. Service just for doing community service is one of the easiest fake activities that I can pick up on and I am sure admissions officers pick up on. Be sincere with your activities and with yourself, but make sure to give back to the community. Admissions officers stress community service because it shows that you have a bigger perspective and that you can really think beyond yourself. Doing an activity just to have it on the resume is 100 percent counter to this philosophy. Do community service in the field you love.

Now that you have a list of activities ready that embody your theme, it is time to hone your approach.

The core of the theme is the **one-sentence approach**. This approach focuses on developing **specificity** in your theme — which automatically raises the level of your theme. Of course, a specific topic can only be reached once general studies are completed. This is why I suggest earlier is better.

In this approach, you can describe your theme in one sentence, completely or completely enough that the audience has a clear image of what exactly you do. I *highly* discourage **boxing** individuals into categories for the long-term, but for this application process our conversation with admissions officers is too short to describe our life's philosophy. Although I think outlook should be part of every great application, another central focus should be on how you plan to integrate your theme into your experience at X University.

Examples of the **one-sentence approach**:

I am a computational linguist and focus on developing mathematical models to describe how vocabulary relates to a writer's sophistication. (This was my **one-sentence approach**).

I am a painter who focuses on using pastels and I have entered several local, statewide, and national art competitions.

I am a historian focusing on studying 17th century Russian social history and I won a statewide contest last year.

I am a mathematician focusing on studying modern algebra and I have entered and won several science fair competitions.

Yes, I realize some of these examples are *high-flying, idealistic* approaches. But the only way you can reach these levels is if you try. In my experiences and my interactions with fellow students, I estimate 80% of my fellow students did not give their *heart* to the process, they did not try and 15% did. This *heart* is detailed in the first chapter:

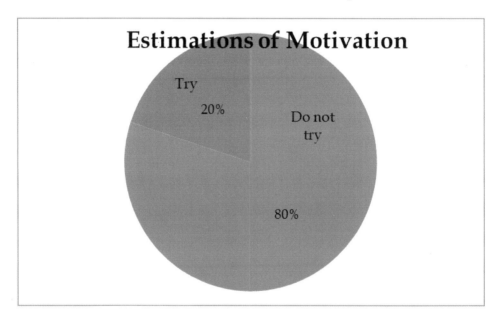

I further estimate that of those 20 percent that tried, 5 percent *dedicated* themselves to the process. Every single one of those 5 percent succeeded. This dedication means prioritizing AND following through almost every single time. It means going above and beyond: not just doing homework, but *embracing* it. You do not have to tell anyone that you are doing this and *embracing* your work — no

they will think you are a "nerd". No, you are not a nerd. You are actually a truly "street-smart" individual who likes to put 100 percent of himself/herself into a task because you know that often effort and result are highly positively correlated.

THE "BIG THING" MYTH

Many admissions counselors and advisors suggest that every student have that "**big thing**". This "thing" could be that research scholarship you won last year or that area of expertise (for example, Colonial History). The myth associated with the "**big thing**" is that it is an achievement or award. I, however, believe that it can *developed* as well — it does not have to be *won*.

I see the importance of having this "thing". For most people, having this large achievement can set you apart from the rest and give you an advantage. For most, if you can get this big thing I definitely would. Some college essay prompts almost specifically ask for this thing:

Describe your most significant personal achievement and how it has shaped you.

These kinds of prompts can be directly answered with your "big thing". Your big achievement also can serve an important function in interviews, as they usually make goods stories. I will give you some examples of these big things so you have an idea of what I mean:

Traditional "Big Things"

1. Representing the USA at an international science conference
2. Winning a nationally-acclaimed essay contest
3. Winning a nationally-acclaimed art contest

Developed "Big Things"

1. Starting a nationally-recognized nonprofit with branches in several states
2. Starting a nationally-successful company
3. Inventing some product or service
4. Your family

The theme usually has most of the following components, each of which is concentrated under a particular *specific* interest.

For example, if you are interested in American history, you may join or create the history club at school, join a history organization, write and publish history essays or submit to competitions, and give back to the community by volunteering your time to teach students about history.

In-school activities

- Clubs
- Organizations

Out-of-school activities

- Community groups
- Regional clubs

Competitions

- Essay contests (for the humanities)
- USAMO, USACO, USABO, Science Fair or other contests

Social Work

- Community Service

FOR SENIORS

This big thing is not absolutely necessary. If you are a senior and are reading this book, do not worry. Develop your theme first, if still possible, and then focus on getting your big achievement. Even if you cannot gain one, try to make your theme resonant. Many of my friends and contemporaries who were successful in the college admissions process did not have a big achievement. I do not want to lie to you, however. The big achievement is an enormous boost in the admissions process and can be the differentiating factor especially among elite schools. But because you are short on time, focus on what you can change. This can-do attitude also differentiates among applicants and comes through in your essays, your interview, and your activities.

FOR NON-SENIORS

You have more time to develop your theme and possibly gain your big achievement. Again, I would first focus on developing a theme and then working towards your big thing. If you develop your theme correctly (entering various competitions and contest) you will naturally be drawn towards nationally-acclaimed and recognized awards. If you win one of these, because you *genuinely* put your heart into the subject matter and the process, you will gain your big achievement. You will usually know when you have gained this achievement.

Once you have gained one, or more than one, big achievement, you will have your theme. To gain these big achievements, months or even years of work go into developing your work. This commitment is why most college applicants do not have one and why it will separate you from the rest. Just be aware of the competitions in your field that are considered "big", and apply for them when you feel you are ready.

I make no promises regarding admissions, but I can firmly say that having a developed theme *with* a big achievement in the same field will help admissions officers identify who you are, what you do, and the level of commitment you are willing to devote to an interest. It will undoubtedly help you in the process and many times is the differentiating factor between acceptances between the different tiers of schools.

Why is this "big thing" important?

First it allows you to clearly develop your theme and often will help you develop your **one-sentence approach**. But I think there is another reason why this "big thing" is important. Gaining or making this achievement is not easy. As I said, it requires commitment. Admissions officers know this fact and if you can show commitment to anything at this level, they know you are ready for most of the college experience: you will be devoted to your classes, to your extracurricular activities, and to anything you put yourself to. This *character trait* is what they are really looking for, in my opinion, and a big achievement is one way to clearly demonstrate vision and willingness to work.

STEPS FOR DEVELOPING A THEME:

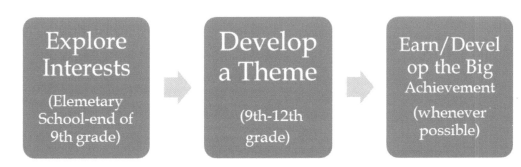

A REAL-LIFE EXAMPLE (my story):

In 5th grade, our science teacher Dr. Dunn made every student do a science fair. I had always had a love for science — mixing soaps in the kitchen and seeing what happened when I experimented with our pets at home. At first, like every other 5th grade student, I did not like the process — especially because I was forced to participate. But halfway through the experience I realized that I *truly* enjoyed doing science research and presenting my work. I decided it was for me and I continued to do science fair projects throughout middle school.

During this time, I did not win any local competitions. I did win every time at my school, but never at the county level. I was not discouraged however — and I am grateful to my parents for encouraging me to continue to pursue my passion. At my second county fair I began to critically analyze which projects were winning and decipher why they were winning. I figured out that I needed to increase my level — the sophistication of my project — in order to have a chance. It is now that I figured out that **specificity** is the key to many things, including science fair projects.

Anyways I dedicated myself to science after 8th grade and decided to *embrace* the process. I decided to develop my theme around science fairs. I did not have any idea about the prestigious competitions at this time but I eventually learned about them and applied to them. I spent countless hours on my project in 9th grade and won

1st place at the county level. This was my first success, and on the success curve, can be considered the catalyst. The level at state was even higher and I did not win. I spent the days following my loss analyzing why again. I spent much of my summer after 10th grade developing a project around computational linguistics and won 1st place at the state level. This was my breakthrough — I started looking at larger competitions and got more opportunities as well. I continued to win at the state level and some national level awards. It took me, realistically, 5 years to learn the process of the science fair judging and what I needed to do. This will probably be true for many of you, as well. It is a long, arduous process. But if you can stick through it, the rewards are big.

The key is to have **vision**. **Vision** is critical in competitions as you can encourage yourself after losses (which are almost inevitable) and push yourself to do better. Admissions officers were once students themselves and many were very successful applicants. They know that this **vision** is necessary and they want students who can dream and who follow through on their dreams. That is why extracurricular activities and competitions are important.

WORK EXPERIENCE

There is much debate surrounding the issue of work experience. Many times I find that students work at local stores to **"resume pad"**. This means that they are working only to put that they have this work experience and do the job for that end only. Often, students do not enjoy working, although the salary they earn (usually hourly pay, around minimum wage) may provide some well-earned pocket change or help the family.

Why does the admissions counselor *want* work

Discipline	Fixated on the money
Value of Money	Short-term gain
Hard Work	"Resume pad"
Real-World Experience	No time to explore other options
Interpersonal Relationships	**Not genuine to self**

experience on an application, or why is it at least viewed as a "good thing to have"? Well, let us look at what it means to work: it means that you have a sense of value for money, that you know how to manage your time, and interact with people in the real world. These kinds of skills are not gained by competing in science fairs or getting straight A's. They are different skill set. For this reason, admissions officers tend to value work experience and the general consensus is that it is a valuable asset on an application or resume. In addition, admissions officers know that some students start exploring degrees in high school. One way to see if a career path is right for you is by interning or working in a related field. Taking the proactive step to do so is admirable and is a great character trait.

If the student *needs* to work for the family, then there is no question: do so. Also mention in your application the purpose of working and what you learned from it: money well-earned, time well-spent, and how to deal with clients are some examples of aspects learned from working in the real world. If you are disadvantaged in this aspect, make sure to mention so in your application. Some universities, such as the University of California, asks specific essay questions geared towards this kind of response.

If you are a student who is trying to **"resume pad"** as a last ditch effort to fill your resume and to gain some work experience, there is no need. College counselors often know that students use this tactic and will read through your approach, especially if this week-long "internship" is the main focus, or **"big thing"**, of your application.

If you are a student who is working, honestly, genuinely, because you are considering the profession you are shadowing or working in, then do it. Demonstrate that real interest in the profession you are working in, and college admissions officers will see that. I know many of my friends, especially students who had a medical inclination, honestly interned because they wanted to see what the profession was like. Still, among these friends some took it as a game and as a **"resume pad"**. MAKE SURE NOT TO DO THAT, it will show in your application in some way, even if you proofread one thousand times. The essay writing process is an irrevocable demonstration of the self—no matter what way you put it.

So, in conclusion, a student should work if they need to for financial reasons or if they are genuinely interested in the field they are shadowing. I feel that for most students summers should be devoted to developing that **"big thing"** and your theme, which for me actually started later than I would have liked: in the summer of 11th grade. This development *can* occur through work experience in a related field (for example, working for a law firm if you are seriously considering becoming a lawyer, combined with joining the school clubs and competing in mock trial events at the state level). Often, however, a theme is developed by extracurricular activities and competitions that are not categorized as work experience. I believe students should start earlier to develop a thorough theme over the years. However, I also believe in not looking back. If you are an 11th grade student or even a 12th grade student, do not worry about what you could have done. That is gone. Focus on the now. Develop what you can.

THE WORK EXPERIENCE MYTH

"Son, you must work somewhere! It is good for admissions and they will see that you know the value of money! Also, you have little time left; at least you can use your time in this manner!"

While this is right in some regards, it is definitely wrong in others. First, the parent seems to be pushing the idea that work experience must be done to "**resume pad**", or fill one's resume with activities for the sake of the resume only. This is wrong and one of the common mistakes that parents, students, and counselors make. Do not work for the resume. It does not work or help.

At the same time, there are some true elements to the statement above. Working does teach you the value of money and other very good lessons. Do not confused the lessons learned from working with the actual effects on a resume. Be yourself, be honest.

If you are working because you truly are considering a career in a related field or want to work, then work! You are being yourself and genuine. If you are working because you must for financial reasons, then work! You are also being genuine and true. If the second case is yours, be sure to recognize this fact on your application and in your essays.

THE RESUME

The resume is critical to your success in communicating your theme and your extracurricular activities. In my experiences, for high school resumes, length is not important beyond the fact that it should not be more than 3 pages (4 perhaps, but I would not make mine 4 pages long). For jobs, resumes are usually one page long, and most of my classmates submitted one page resumes for college, but length does not seem to matter. The resume is the document that should clearly communicate your theme and should show *effort*. At the same time, if you want to appear professional — real resumes are often 1 page at maximum. It is entirely your choice, but from my experiences and from those of my peers I have found that length is not entirely critical — just do not make it a book.

Just like with your theme, the resume is beautiful because it allows creativity. At the same time, this creativity must also exhibit substance.

First, your resume should be computer-generated. I have printed my resume more than 100 times in the past year. Think of your big thing, if you have one. You want this to be on the first page. The key to a highly successful resume is to communicate the *level* of involvement you are in with your activities. The higher, the better, but please be HONEST with your activities. I will tell you I was and I know some that were not — they paid the price two or three years later. Please be HONEST, admissions officers can see right through a façade, they have many times before.

In my experiences, if you are aiming at elite institutions (refer to School-Centric Approach for more information on how many/which schools to apply to) you should have some kind of *state* or *national* level achievement or achievements. I know this is not absolutely necessary, but it will always help. This approach is for most students and for those who do not have legacy or fall in another category. I have found that this approach works more often than others.

There are many ways to approach this *state* or *national* level of success. If you have a slew of statewide achievements and one national achievement, that is very good. If you have one widely recognized nationwide achievement (for example, Intel Science Talent Search), you will be in good position. However, I have found that if you have this kind of achievement, you often have other statewide achievements and maybe nationwide recognition. This takes us back to the success curve: the more you involve yourself, the more you try, the more you will succeed.

If you are aiming at very good institutions, a slew of local achievements and a statewide achievement will be enough for an outstanding resume. I would still recommend participating in several statewide competitions — the more, the better. The gap between very good institutions and top institutions is becoming smaller (sometimes separated just by the fact that some are private institutions and others public, which means more individual attention).

If you are aiming at other institutions, I would still recommend coming up with a plan of action and applying to several local competitions and a few statewide competitions. Applying can never hurt, and *anyone* can win these competitions. If you win some of these, you will have an extremely good chance of being accepted. Apply with all your heart.

Whatever level of institution you are planning on applying to, the key is to apply for competitions. This **competition-centric approach** is concrete and if you win, allows you create a solid resume. Competitions usually have succinct names that can be transferred to resumes and also require the effort that admissions officers are looking for, especially the prestigious competitions. Here is a flowchart in regards to competitions and the **competition-centric approach**:

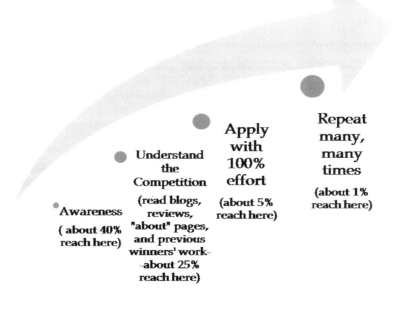

Repeat many, many times

(about 1% reach here)

Apply with 100% effort

(about 5% reach here)

Understand the Competition

(read blogs, reviews, "about" pages, and previous winners' work--about 25% reach here)

Awareness

(about 40% reach here)

The key is persistence in applying for competitions. I lost more times than I won and most people I know had the same record. But I kept applying—I was discouraged because I put my heart into the competitions but I did not stop. This is true for most people.

I also started noticing the *same people* at all my competitions. I specialized in science fairs. I realize that I saw the same people because we all applied for every competition we could find and embraced each one completely. I started winning competitions only after the first few years of understanding the logistics of each competition, what each competition looked for, and what niche I needed to develop in order to win. Do not worry if you do not win the first time, the second time, or even the third. I won during my fourth competition because I finally understood the process. This is the success curve for competitions:

Let me explain this graph. For many of your first attempts, you may not succeed. I lost my first five science fair competitions. But eventually, if you stick with your

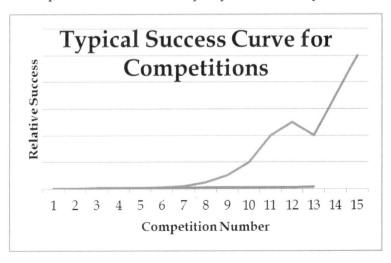

desired **area of concentration**, you will find what specific competitions are looking for. You will learn the system and how to eloquently *show* your dedication to the judges — it is just like the resume and the entire application process. Competitions and the application process are about *showing* your passion and this is why admissions officers look at your extracurricular activities. They require the same set of skills needed in college and throughout life.

So you start winning competitions — starting at the local levels. Be grateful for every step. Soon you may be winning fourth or third place at state competitions. You are ecstatic. But during your next competition you do not even make it out of the local competition. That is the hump on competition 13. This hump happens with most of us. It is a result of the luck that is associated with most competitions and the subjectivity that is inherent in judging. DO NOT BE DISCOURAGED! Continue doing what you know will work and what you love. You may eventually hit the success associated with competition 15.

Remember this graph is the model success curve. I firmly believe that any individual can succeed at anything — some call me a dreamer. But I truly think anything is possible if the *student* puts his/her mind to the task and devotes himself/herself to the area of study. Sometimes, however, students do not win any competitions and time runs short. In this case, I would encourage students to try another area that they think they would be good at. Diversify until you are successful. Do this approach only if you are running short on time (say, you are in the middle of 11th grade with no achievements yet). When you win one, continue on this path and in this area.

Once you have completed several competitions and hopefully done well in some of these, you are ready to start compiling your resume. First, some advice:

1. You will be entering many competitions. In an electronic document, we will call it the **resume-builder**, which is saved to many different locations because it is so important, write down every single competition you enter. Write down the date you entered and perhaps attach the application you filed for the application. This organizational hint came in handy when I started creating my resume after four years of activity.

    a. You can keep this organizational document in chronological order easily — if you enter each competition soon after applying the document will be in order. This is useful for looking for a theme and the progression of your success in a particular field (your **niche**).

    b. Keep track of how you did — perhaps also write down some ideas that the judges gave you for your future competitions.

2. Do you research about the competitions to increase your awareness (Step 1) several months ahead of time — this is especially critical for larger

competitions. Sometimes they have unique rules and limitations that need to be prepared for.

    a.   This approach will also allow you enough time to apply with all of your ability and your heart to each competition. More time on the application usually results in higher quality and a better representation of your work and your commitment.

Now you are ready to start creating your resume. This creation can be done at any time. There are two approaches:

1. Compile it as you go along — develop it along with your **resume-builder**.
   a. This approach saves you stress down the road, when you are working on your essays. Remember, however, to use a format that you will be comfortable with in the next few years. Only content should be added — formats should be changed few times if any because it is quite time-consuming and takes away time from doing other endeavors.
2. Compile it during the beginning of 12th grade (preliminary draft: early August-early September)
   a. This approach allows you to focus on your tasks during earlier grades but makes you do more work along with your essays and the course load of 12th grade.

The resume is very similar to a website in terms of form and function:

1. Content—The high school resume highlights a central theme supported by your extracurricular activities—the focus are your extracurricular activities and your competitions
    a. Make sure that you succinctly highlight the titles of competitions and your placement. The eyes should be drawn towards these elements first.
    b. Your activities should either be the first or second aspect that readers see (either above or below your competitions)
        i. Highlight your leadership positions and/or any significant sub-activities or changes you made in the organization
    c. Your work experience—unless it is more significant than your competitions and activities (which it could be but usually is not) should be next
    d. Your "other" interests should be next, such as your hobbies or anything that could set you apart
        i. What do you do in your free time that is constructive and productive? Add these activities here
    e. Your education—such as the school you went to—should be next

Remember this is a generalized format for the resume. Your own resume can be different but remember that the focus should be what you have done outside of school and how that demonstrates your theme. Make sure content is more prominent than style every time, but remember that style can be an appealing factor that demonstrates personality and a pop. Admissions officers get enough white, single-paged resumes. At the same time, they will see right through a resume with no substance and beautiful form. As you can see, it is a delicate balance that you really must work on.

Here are a few programs that you can use to create your resume:

1. Microsoft Word
2. Adobe Photoshop
3. Adobe CreatePDF
4. Adobe Dreamweaver
5. Any coding software

To give you an idea of the **resume-builder**, I have created a sample below, which can be done in Microsoft Word. This **resume-builder** will help when it comes time to create a full resume and during the interview process, whether it be for college or for a job. By having specific points of life documented, you can show who you are through individual events.

Of course, you need to have a cohesive story first and then apply these specific events to give evidence.

Here is a sample **resume-builder**:

5th grade "Mavericks" Soccer MVP

- Played forward
- Won 11 out of 15 games
- Enjoyed the competitive spirit and teamwork and especially the game against the "Hawks" September 10th, 2011

7th grade Science Fair Winner

Looking at Newton's Laws Through the Rollercoaster

- Put abstract online and competed an abstract, problem, experiment, results, and conclusion
- Was mentored by science teacher Ms. Walker
- Enjoyed learning the science and physics, maybe I can consider it in the future

RECOMMENDATIONS

Recommendations are one of the more important aspects of the application process. These are letters written by teachers, coordinators of extracurricular activities, counselors, or any other person who knows you well and has worked with or so has seen you work.

Let us take the admissions officer's perspective. They want to see how you function daily from the eyes, the judgment, and the experience of another individual. These recommendations help admissions officers see how you are beyond the resume and the scores. It helps them decipher your personality and your drive, Applicant Aspect 3 (presented at the end of the book).

With this in mind, who should you ask a recommendation from? Consider that you want a diverse set of perspectives that show that you work diligently and have vision. This would result in getting recommendations from teachers to show your academic drive, from individuals involved in your extracurricular activities (if possible), and mentors. You want to give sources that are as unbiased as possible, so any kind of family member should not be included. Some applications ask for a family member's particular viewpoint of you or a classmate's view of you (Duke University and Dartmouth University have done this in the past). In only this case should you ask peers or family members for recommendations — in my opinion.

To get an idea of what the admissions officers are trying to understand about you read through the

Supplement provided for recommendations. These have boxes and ask recommenders to rate you on specific items. If you are in any grade below 11th, you have an advantage. Position yourself in the class, *embrace* the class, so that these character traits are visible. Usually, demonstration of these traits means active participation and true interest in the subject material, which usually results in better grades and a successful classroom experience.

Many students get these recommendations at the beginning or even in the middle of 12th grade. Do NOT do this. I repeat, do not wait this long to get your recommendations if you still have that choice. If you are a senior right now, do not worry about what you cannot change — make sure you get the letters though. I would suggest getting your recommendations from 11th and 12th grade teachers. If you had an exceptional experience with a 10th grade instructor, ask him/her. I did ask one 10th grade teacher to give me a recommendation. If you did not have great experiences with enough of your 11th grade teachers and want to get one from a 12th grade teacher, make sure that you develop your relationship before December. You will need the letters for Regular Decision mid-December before Winter Break.

How many people should I ask? Well, that really depends on how many your universities are asking for. Most ask for two recommendations, some ask for three. Make sure that you get the right number. There is another approach: ask for many recommendations. If the teacher allows you to look at the recommendation letter, you can craft your combination of letters to fit a theme. Remember, if you are honest with yourself and the process, this thematic flow will come naturally.

Also, be sensitive to the recommender. Some want you to proofread their letters and others want to send it sealed without you reading them. Be respectful to their choice and ask them which method they prefer. Often, you can guess based on the personality of the recommender — but still ask. If you have many recommenders who want you to proofread and are casual about you reading or even sending their letters you can ask them to selective send theirs to certain universities to make combinations of recommendations that you send to different colleges.

Remember to thank each recommender. This is a sign of maturity and appreciation. I would recommend a hand-written note to each recommender that you personally deliver perhaps with a small token and some nice words. Teachers are usually underappreciated. This touch can be used in many aspects of life and demonstrates true understanding and maturity.

"THE INTERNATIONAL"

AP or IB Tests

Taking AP or IB tests are critical for showing academic excellence. Many schools outside of the United States do not offer AP/IB courses, so often students self-study from test books and take the tests at certified schools. Some schools outside of the US, often called "international schools", do offer these courses. For AP/IB tests, you must take the exam at a registered school. The general rule of thumb is to take as many AP/IB tests as you can while maintaining good grades.

There are a few test-preparation book companies that I recommend for AP/IB: Barron's, Princteon Review, Kaplan, and Peterson's. Barron's usually has the most amount of material covered in the first part of the book, often more than the test covers. It is important, if you study with Barron's, to know what to study. The tests are also more difficult than the other review books, but if you can do very well on these practice tests you will have more than enough knowledge for the actual exams. That is how Barron's has been designed. Princeton Review, on the other hand, is often the lightest of material covered and the exams tend to be slightly easier than the actual exams. Princeton Review is good for taking exams and practicing test-taking strategies such as time management, but the material on the actual exam is usually more in-depth. Kaplan is like Princeton Review, and is good for practicing terms and concepts while also focusing on test-taking habits. Taking these kinds of tests help you stay on top of the material by jogging your memory but may not be fully adequate. Finally, Peterson's is especially good for history courses, but the writing style and the verbose style of the book is not everyone's style of studying. You should read some of the book when you are at the bookstore before purchasing. Ultimately, like I did, I recommend a combination of these books and more that you can find. That way you can practice both the material and test-taking strategies and understand different kinds of questions made by different test-makers.

SAT/ACT

Studying for the SAT or ACT outside of the US can be quite different. Many tutors in other countries may even lead students incorrectly. The goal is test-taking. If you take enough exams, you will eventually cover all the material that is needed on the exam and know how it feels to sit down and take a multi-hour exam.

There are many types of books that you can get for SAT/ACT preparation, including Barron's, Princeton Review, and Kaplan. The same principles above for AP/IB tests applies to SAT preparation: Barron's often contains harder mathematics than appear on the SAT I or SAT II Subject Test. The key is to take as many tests as you can. On top of that, it is critical to iterate: learn from your mistakes. If the test takes you four hours to complete, take one hour to review what you got *right* and wrong. Take the tests in simulated settings, do not take sections. Do not give yourself more time than you have during your practice tests. If you can do all of these things, and you are able to take 30 full-length practice exams, you will be in good shape for the actual exams.

For vocabulary, I recommend *Direct Hits*, which is precise and many of the words tend to show up on the SAT. Start learning these words as soon as you can, and try to incorporate them into your SAT/ACT essays as well. For general preparation, there is the "Blue Book", the Official SAT Tests that are occasionally released. I recommend students to take these exams near the end of their preparation so they are subconsciously prepared for the actual exam's content in a very similar fashion.

To find a test center, you can visit www.collegeboard.com and locate the nearest testing center. If you have to travel a distance, you should make the trip — the SAT/ACT is one of the most important parts of your application. At the same time, it is only one part of your application. Schools in the US look at your extracurricular activity *depth* over *breadth* and your scores.

SAT II

SAT II tests are standard and two or three are often required. I recommend students to always take three SAT II tests at least. You can choose which ones colleges see, as well. Often, take the tests during or right after you have taken the corresponding class. So if you are taking the Chemistry SAT II, I recommend students to take the exam when they take Chemistry or right after. The SAT II Subject Tests are more subject-oriented and more academic in nature. There are many test preparation books that cater specifically to these exams, including Barron's and The

Official SAT II Subject Tests, which are occasionally released. I give high recommendation to taking these released practice exams near the end of your preparation so that you know where you stand and are prepared for very similar material on the actual test day.

There is a unique set of students that must be addressed separately: the international student applying to schools within the US. Especially in today's "flattening" world, the world is become more global every second. Students from India, China, South Korea, South Africa, Japan, Brazil, and everywhere else are looking to apply to US schools. The general philosophy outlined above, as well as the basic tests (SAT/ACT), and extracurricular strengths are all equally applicable for the international student. In the end, schools in the United States are looking for *talented*, *driven*, and *passionate* individuals who want to make a difference in their lifetime in whatever they do. The process they use to identify the students they think fit these qualities has to be very similar, regardless of where the students are from as they characteristics are internal. That being said, location does indeed place a role in college admissions, because admissions officers realize that location plays a role in developing an individual, their personality, and their view on life.

Where to apply?

If finances could hinder your application to many US schools, choosing which schools to apply to also can become an art. The same principles in the other chapter of this book apply to the international student, but perhaps I can give particular note here. Diversify where you apply:

do not apply to only schools with single-digit acceptance rates. Include great schools like Emory and University of Pennsylvania, which currently have a keen knack for taking international students and there is a great culture there of internationals. These schools are some of the few remaining with need-blind admission for international students, meaning that students are not at a disadvantage if they mark the "seeking financial aid" box.

There is no wrong school to apply to. Unlike universities outside of the US, US universities cater to all kinds of students. Liberal arts schools are always trying to attract science talent, and are often very generous with merit-based aid as well. I applied to a few of these kinds of schools and received aid and individual attention because of my unusual interests. At the same time, schools like MIT prize students coming with a more humanities-sided aspect, although it is possible to say that most students at MIT and Caltech are there for the mathematics and sciences. You may feel out of place at these two schools, but most everywhere else you will not feel that way. US universities are very liberal when it comes to which subjects students take — the prestige of the university is not a factor of getting into a particular program as much as the people there.

First, if you are an international student reading this, I do think that you should also read the other parts of this book thoroughly: they also apply equally to you. The admissions officers are looking for potential and drive and that is something that is universal. The ways that they search for these aspects is the same regardless of applicant:

essay, tests, and interviews if possible. Most if not all of this book is applicable to you. This section is dedicated to the differences that exist for you, but I wanted to make the rest of this book also useful for you.

There seems to be misconception among all students, and *especially* international students, that visiting a school is essential to admission. *This misconception is not true.* Although visiting a school does show interest, it is not needed and it is possible to learn even more about a school from searching websites correctly. This searching means looking at YouTube official videos of a particular school, talking to students and faculty, and reading on specific department pages of a university.

International students applying to the United States often should take an extra examination called the TOEFL (Test of English as a Foreign Language). Although many schools do not require it, such as Caltech and Yale, they are always recommended — which means, you should do it. Consider the admission officer: he wants to assess your potential and ability to thrive academically. Knowing that one has command in English, especially if the student is going to attend a US school with primarily English speakers, should not be the focus or concern. One way to relax these concerns is to prove command through the TOEFL.

In particular, many students take the TOEFL iBT, which is a four hour examination conducted online that tests "ability to use and understand English at the university level... [evaluating] how well you combine your listening, reading, speaking and writing skills to perform

academic tasks." (http://www.ets.org/toefl/ibt/about/)
Often, as Yale states on its website, this test is not used as
an *admissions factor* but as a bar to assess language use —
high TOEFL scores would be useful but are not necessarily
equivalent to high SAT, ACT, or SAT subject test scores.
Although I cannot speak from individual account, many of
my colleagues suggest that the TOEFL is used just to
screen applicants for the ability to use the English
language and be comfortable in it. There may be a
misconception here that high TOEFL scores are a must, but
from talking in specific to Stanford students from South
Korea, Vietnam, Russia, and China this does not seem to
be true. Instead of focusing all energy on gaining a near
perfect or perfect score on the TOEFL, the general
consensus among students is to focus on the SAT and
related **academic tests.** The TOEFL would fall under a
different category: **bar-setting tests.** Unfortunately, two
myths appear from misinformed perceptions of both of
these tests.

Discussions with international classmates attending
Stanford from Jamaica, South Korea, China, India, Russia,
South Africa, and Chile form the basis for much of the
following perceptions of exam scores and other principles
for "the international". These students attend many
schools including Harvard University, Stanford
University, many of the University of California schools,
Princeton, and Yale.

From their opinions, it seems that what admission
officers are looking for are very similar to what they look
for from domestic applicants. In the end, what they search

for is the same: academic ability, personality (whatever it may be, although it must be there) that is developed through extracurricular activities, individuality, drive, and **perspective**. SAT/ACT, SAT subject tests, AP scores, GPA, and recommendation letters cover much of the academic portion for the admissions officers. They are standardized tests for a reason — they are now taken across the world and wanted by most US institutions. In addition, admission officers look for **perspective** — the ability to add individuality to a scenario, class, or other event from personal experience, outlook on life, and upbringing. Often, this is where the international applicant is a little different from the domestic applicant. Sometimes, an extracurricular activity can play into **perspective** especially if the activity has been done since childhood. But often, upbringing and location can play into this **perspective**. How does your upbringing in Tokyo differentiate you from those born and raised in Los Angeles? What cultural norms have become part of you and affect how you interact with others. Is there something that can be gained from your point of view in interactions with those brought up in Los Angeles? These are the kinds of questions that the international student should contemplate before starting the admissions process or very early on in the process. Contemplate where you stand for admissions officers and how you see yourself in the American system. This **perspective** is often gained by admissions officers through essay question answers — the essay *is* a representation of who we are, after all.

Now the "international" ballpark can vary dramatically. I have classmates who lived in England and other international locations but came to the United States every summer and many times during the year to visit friends and family. I have other classmates who have never entered the United States prior to coming to college. I am sure that admissions officers take this into account and are probably able to discern an applicant's exposure to American culture through their writing style and outlook. Wherever you fall on this scale, there is one thing to remember: BE YOURSELF. Do not worry about what the admission officers think, focus on who you really are, what you believe in, and your true outlook on whatever questions are posed in the essays.

There are some conceptions that admissions to US schools from the international pool are more difficult than admissions to US schools from within. This may be true — but no one can really be sure as these kinds of admissions statistics are not released. In addition, even if they were, even more myths would be generated. These kinds of statistics — in general — must be viewed in context. Are there more misinformed or under-prepared applicants applying from outside the United States, which would lower admissions rates but not make it necessarily "harder" to get in? Vice versa, are those applying from outside the United States more aware and more driven, as a group, than that group that applies from within the United States? Such judgments on large groups of people cannot be made with precision, and I will not try to make them. From my conversations with successful international students, it seems that most are extremely aware of the global world and the impact that a US education can have on their future. They seem to be highly capable of

academic pursuits and they definitely add a unique flavor
to the dorm dynamic, the classroom atmosphere, and the
university setting. Eventually, I do not even know the
difference: everyone becomes part of the community. This
is perhaps one of the greatest aspects of the college
experience: a group cohesion that develops with university
classmates and especially within freshman living spaces.

Many international students go to international
schools where they were exposed to the American
education system primarily and also other education
systems in a formalized fashion. For these students, it is
not uncommon for the goal to be to go to an American
university. Many classmates from Europe that attend
American schools now have done this and were very
aware of exams such as the SAT and subject tests. These
students tell me that the process was very similar for them
as it was for me—the tests, the classes, and the atmosphere
was similar but in a different location. They do have
different perspectives, but academically they were
surrounded by peers also trying to gain admissions in the
US or other countries and have an overlap of perspective
with domestic applicants. If you fall in this category, know
that much of the experience is the same, although critical
differences exist because of location. Still, vision is
necessary, because only some of the best or most ambitious
students from these students come to the United States for
school. You probably know many of the tests you will
need to take. But for the essays and **perspective** be very
careful to not overstress what you hope the admissions
officers want to see and undervalue who you really are.
Often, I find that students in this category can be prone to

myths because they are pressured to apply to American schools. Be yourself. Apply where you want to and where you see yourself. If that is in the US, then apply. If it is in Europe or somewhere else, let it be there. If you do not know, perhaps apply everywhere. That is the safest approach.

Others were one of the few to apply to schools in the United States. One particular classmate from South Korea was one of fifteen to take the SAT from his high school. His year had about 1,000 students. For him, he had to have the *vision* to know about US schools, know what it took to apply (such as independently researching the SAT), and successfully writing essays in a foreign language as well as proving mastery via the TOEFL. As we can see, drive and vision were necessary just for him to apply. Getting accepted is another matter and proves his vision and his ability to successfully convey passion and himself through the process. This is why I often have much respect for international students coming to US schools and why some people think that the admissions process is harder for international students: those coming are often motivated and visionary. If you fall in this category, know that you will have to do "extra" work identifying what you must do—which I have hopefully lessened with this book—and that you will need drive. If you accept these two facts, then the process should be straightforward. Be yourself. Have passion. Do the necessary tests.

Finally, there is another category of students who apply: students who recently moved from international locations and attend schools within the US but have a strong international perspective due to many years living abroad. To my surprise, I found many of my classmates have experience living abroad. For example, some lived in China for 10 years then moved to the United States for the end of middle school and for all of high school. These individuals usually have a unique perspective — they have experienced two kinds of cultures but are also integrated into the American mindset and school system. If you fall in this category, consider your perspective an advantage. You truly have an international perspective. Write who you really think you are in your essays, again the same principle. If you think your exposure in the US has been more defining than your time elsewhere, say that. Be yourself, stress your unique experiences if they make up who you are, and do the necessary exams (which you will know what they are because you are in the US education system).

On the next page, I have given another myth of college admissions for the international student.

THE TOEFL MYTH

Many students applying from international locations to US schools are required to take the TOEFL examination, especially for competitive institutions. The general attitude of perfectionism sometimes carries over to the TOEFL.

"You must score perfect on the TOEFL!"

From conversations with my international classmates, it seems that they do not feel this way. Many scored exceptionally on **academic tests** such as the SAT and ACT but did not feel it necessary to also score in the 99.98th percentile on the TOEFL. The TOEFL's purpose is to credit the ability to converse at university level in the English language, not to discern academic potential or ability. Although a high score would never hurt, it may not be *as* necessary as a high score on the SAT, for example. With the experiences of my classmates and what I feel, I think that if I had to choose to either devote more time to the SAT or the TOEFL, I would definitely choose the SAT. Look at the purpose of each exam and consider which the admissions officers would want to know more about: the ability to converse in English or the ability to learn, develop, analyze, and synthesize quickly.

Student A: I need to score 2300 on my SAT and get a 4.0 unweighted GPA and participate in the only extracurricular activity that everyone does: the Computing Olympiad. There is no other way.

Student B: I do need to score relatively well and try my best on the SAT, but the key is to have the right perspective. I can start my own clubs because I read that many students do that in other countries, maybe I can talk about that experience in my essays.

PART 3: ALONG THE JOURNEY

THE SCHOOL-CENTRIC APPROACH

As important as all the essays, the resume-building, and the interview are the choice of schools you are applying to. The number and caliber of schools you are applying to will help determine how much of a commitment you are willing to put into the application process and into yourself. Each individual must decide for himself/herself how many essays he/she wants to write and how many interviews he/she wants to conduct. There are three strategies which involve the general **school-centric approach**. The **school-centric approach** focuses the student on applying to schools that he/she can *truly* picture himself/herself at. Do not apply to schools because you are forced to. Apply to them because you want to.

The three strategies within this approach:

1. **High-output approach**: In this approach, the student applies to many schools (typically over 15). The idea here is to have a wider range of choices (hopefully) when the results come back and also to be able to apply to schools with different atmospheres and in different calibers.

2. **Medium-output approach**: In this approach, the student has focused on a good number of schools to apply to. He/she puts all his/her effort into the process and truly wants to attend every school on his/her list. There is, however, less room for diversification among calibers and atmospheres with this approach.

3. **Low-output approach**: In this approach, which I think is rare and should only be taken in very specific cases, the student has decided on a small number of schools (perhaps 5) that he/she wants to apply to. Caliber and atmosphere are not of concern here—rather something about each institution makes it special to the student. This approach is extremely risky and I would not advise it.

I personally took the **high-output approach**. I felt that I could see myself actually living and working in a number of atmospheres and therefore a number of schools. I am also the type to want backup in my decisions and I figured that if I apply to more schools, I may have more choices or choices at all.

It is apparent that applying to more schools means that you have more essays, more reviewing, more interviews, and more overall work. But the payoff is the possibility of having more choices and perhaps getting into more top-tier universities with low acceptance rates. Each student should decide on their own how much work to put in. I would take the same approach again because I feel like I gave my heart to academics for several years and I wanted to see how I would fare among many admissions decisions and if institutions thought I was the right fit for them. It was both a move for self-discovery and analysis and one that fits my personality.

Whatever approach you take, excluding the **low-output approach**, I would recommend following the classic **three-tier method**. In this method, students apply to three levels of schools in order to diversify. It is very similar to modern portfolio theory, in which individuals are also dealing with risk and uncertainty.

1. **"Reach" schools**: These are your dream schools. Usually they have exceptionally low acceptance rates and are considered elite institutions for one or many subjects. My advice is to please apply to these schools. Even if you do not think you can make it based on your scores and such, your essays might just click with an admissions officer. That is really all it sometimes takes. If you do think you might be fit for these kinds of schools, take the **high-output approach** and apply to all or many of these schools. See how you fare.
2. **"In range" schools**: These are schools that you think you could fairly easily get assimilated into, in terms of academics and the level of other students. This bar is different for everyone. In any approach, apply to some of these schools and see how you do. These days, the difference between **"In range" schools** and **"Reach" schools** is getting blurred.
3. **"Safety" schools**: These schools are those which you think you have a very good chance of getting accepted to. Be careful! Do not underestimate any school, in my opinion. These schools can include local institutions and some state schools. In any approach, apply to at least some of these institutions.

Diversification is the key in the admissions process, especially if you are considering a **high-output approach**.

Realize that LUCK plays a critical part in all admissions processes, and that you may be rejected from your dream school.

If I were to recommend based off my experiences and from the results of my classmates, I would say most students should take the **high-output approach**, especially if you are considering top-notch schools with low acceptance rates. Do more work earlier and get more choices later. You may not enough the process now, but trust me, you will be pleased with yourself later. Even if the results do not come out perfectly — you may have had even fewer choices if you tried another approach. It is the safest approach but also requires the most work. I would still recommend this approach — it worked for me and for many of my classmates.

EARLY ACTION AND EARLY DECISION

Some institutions have early action and early decision programs. Early Action means that students apply earlier to these institutions and also get notification of acceptance, waitlist, or denial earlier (usually in December or early January). The difference between Early Action and Early Decision is the binding nature of the latter—if you are accepted to an Early Decision school, you are obliged to attend.

There are many theories surrounding both of these methods. Acceptance rates do tend to be higher for both of these programs but the reasons for this are numerous. I believe that the theories are statistical extrapolations and do not have very solid basis. I consider them instead hypotheses. For example, some suggest that applying Early Action will give you *better* chances of admission, and supporters point to the higher acceptance rates. However, I think that the students who apply Early Action are more inclined to attend that institution, in general, than the group that applies Regular Decision. They tend to be more motivated and organized because they choose to apply earlier. The rate of admission may be higher just because the batch of students is a better fit for that institution. Also, athletes and legacy are said to be encouraged to apply Early Action or Early Decision and the recruitment process skews the acceptance rate for other niches.

In any case, I believe that if you decide to apply Early Action you should be very motivated to actually attend that institution. Some are Restrictive Early Action programs, which means that you can only apply to that institution early. For these particular programs, I think that students in the academic niche or actually any niche need to demonstrate an unusual desire to attend that particular institution. They want to get to know earlier perhaps because this is their dream school. I shy away from using dream school (See Dream School Predicament), but many students who do apply under these kinds of programs apply to the school that they have always wanted to attend.

If you are considering Early Decision, you must be set on attending that institution if you are accepted. Not only must you demonstrate an unusual desire to attend that institution, you must *know* deep down that you really want to go there. If you are considering one of these programs, make sure that you really want to attend that school. I would take extra time to think about this before applying.

THE DREAM SCHOOL PREDICAMENT

Now what if you have that one school you want to go to that you have wanted to go to for all of your life? Some students have what I call the **dream school predicament**. Dreams are never a problem. I think every student should be a dreamer actually. But I think that the application process should not focus on one particular school—even if you have legacy to that school, live close to it, or have parents at a particular institution. I firmly believe that although every individual may have leanings towards particular schools, he/she should try to be as unbiased as he/she can be until the results come. Once you have the acceptance letters in hand, you can then start judging where you want to go. The only other time that you should judge is when deciding where to apply. Every school that you apply to should be your dream school at the time when you are applying, interviewing, and writing your essays. You have *chosen* to apply to particular schools because you feel each one has something special and that you can *actually* see yourself there. Apply to each as if it were your dream school. That is how I approached it and later I found that many of my friends who were successful also approached it. Be impartial during the time of applications. Start judging institutions only once you have acceptances and when you can start reevaluating where you would best see yourself.

If you have the **dream school predicament** or a set of schools (perhaps the Ivy League schools) that you have a strong inclination to go to, first try and clear your mind. Think that you should not attach yourself to any school over another until you have acceptance letters. Your emotions are based on hypotheticals until then, and so you should refrain from creating a **choice list of schools**. This list will inevitably create inclinations for particular schools which is what you are trying to avoid.

For every student in the application process, fellow students, teachers, and parents or friends' parents will ask you about your choice list. Tell them that you do not have such a list. This is the approach I took. I told them I did not have a **number one school** or anything like that. I actually did not either. Even if you do, by telling yourself that you do not over and over it will dull your inclinations for particular schools. Try your equal best on all of your applications.

Once you have cleared your mind and convinced yourself that you should not have a list of schools ordered by preference, you are ready to start applying.

WHICH SCHOOLS?

Choosing which schools to apply to is an art of its own. To help, we have developed the **red-yellow-green method** of choosing colleges and of organizing them in some fashion. The Common Application allows you to apply to a maximum of 20 schools and a minimum of 1 school. These are schools that use the Common Application, so your total could exceed 20 if you apply to schools that have their own application forms.

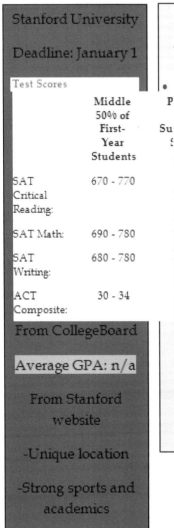

Stanford University

Deadline: January 1

Test Scores

	Middle 50% of First-Year Students
SAT Critical Reading:	670 - 770
SAT Math:	690 - 780
SAT Writing:	680 - 780
ACT Composite:	30 - 34

From CollegeBoard

Average GPA: n/a

From Stanford website

-Unique location

-Strong sports and academics

UCSB

Deadline: November 30

- Test Scores -- 25th / 75th Percentile
- SAT Critical Reading: 530 / 650
- SAT Math: 550 / 670
- SAT Writing: 540 / 660

From About.com

Average GPA: 4.08 weighted

From UCSB website

-Unique location

-Strong research

-Great social scene

University of Idaho

Deadline: February 1

	Middle 50% of First-Year Students
SAT Critical Reading:	480 - 600
SAT Math:	490 - 610
SAT Writing:	460 - 570
ACT Composite:	20 - 26

From CollegeBoard

Average GPA: 3.3 weighted

From Princeton Review

-Good value

-Unique athletic training degree

To give you an example of what this method is, above is a sample of three schools that are categorized via the **red-yellow-green method**.

Red schools are **reach schools**, for any student they are dream schools, regardless of SAT score or GPA. These schools consist of Ivy League schools, Stanford, and similar schools. Yellow schools are **in-range schools**, meaning that according to our statistics and our beliefs, this is a school that we are suited for, just numerically. Finally, green schools are **safety schools**, schools which we would attend if we did not get into any other school.

This method of coloring is solely based off of GPA and SAT. It is meant only to get you a sense of the kinds of schools you are applying to and what to expect. Try to be skeptical instead of optimistic — place schools in red over yellow if you are unsure, so that you do not get your hopes higher. Also, list interesting aspects of the school, aspects that you personally like and will later write about perhaps in the essay process.

Although the number of schools that are green, yellow, and red vary for each student and the total number of schools that you apply to also varies, the safest route is to apply to the near upper limit. You can apply for fee waivers if you cannot afford the application fee, and then the only difference is hard work and the number of essays you write. I highly encourage students to write and read as much as they can, and the application process is an intense time of writing. By applying to more schools, you may have more choices, which would pay the dividends for your hard work later on.

In terms of specific schools, students should always have at least 1 green school in the worst case scenario. Everything else is subject to the student. Most students end up having an equal number of yellow and red schools, or slightly more yellow than red schools. This choice of the number of each kind of school is based on you.

Finally, I encourage students to actually get folders with these colors and print the **cover page** that has been shown above. Eventually, students should print out other interesting material from each school's website. If you are writing about why you like a university, for example, go to its research page and find a particular faculty member who does research you like. In addition to writing about that faculty member, print out one of their academic papers and put it in this folder for the school. Each school should have some kind of information like this. In this way, you have personalized folders for each school, which you can look over before your interview to remind you of unique qualities of the school you are applying to and to make the whole process streamlined, especially for students applying to many schools.

Please see "The Presentation" for more on this topic and how developing personalized folders plays into the interview process and later stages.

PRE-PROFESSIONAL PROGRAMS

Pre-professional programs, such as accelerated 7 or 8 year dental or medical programs, are common in the United States and sometimes should be considered an option for students. These programs are often very competitive to gain entrance into, and require an average GPA to be maintained throughout the college career. Some of the programs waive the DAT (Dental Admissions Test) or the MCAT (Medical College Admissions Test), but some still require it, but with a relatively lower score as the requirement to stay in the program.

Usually I recommend these programs to students who are set on being involved in the medical field, but be wary, many students believe they want this path but end up changing. Often students accepted to these programs are already strong in Chemistry and Biology, and have exhibited great scores on the SAT II exams for these subjects. Some schools require either the Chemistry or Biology SAT II, and some even ask for a foreign language SAT II in order to show a breadth of academic ability. Successful applicants in these programs also usually have solid SAT I and GPA scores, usually well above the school's average. Be sure to check the school's website prior to taking these exams so that you know which to take and which they recommend. For these programs, completing the recommended subjects is quite a good idea.

Students who apply to these programs should know they are very competitive and plan for back-up programs. By applying for accelerated programs you also must apply to the undergraduate program, so in the case you are not accepted to the accelerated program, you may be accepted to the college. In some cases, admittance to an honors college is a prerequisite for being considered for the accelerated program. Because the Common Application currently allows 20 schools maximum, every accelerated program you apply for counts as one of your options, so planning must be done (refer to "Which Schools? for more).

University of Connecticut	Case Western University
Brown University	Tufts University
Boston University	University of the Pacific
New York University	Penn State University

Think very carefully before applying to these programs, and consider how many to apply to before you

do. Above is an example list of some universities offering accelerated programs.

There is no need to get hearts set on a pre-professional program. They are very difficult to get into and not the right choice for every applicant. It is always possible to go to a 4 year undergraduate university and then get into medical or dental school. Be cautionary when applying, and cautiously optimistic.

FINANCIAL AID

Financial aid covers three many areas: loans, grants, work-study, and tax savings. Most of the time, students and parents tend to focus on loans because of their widespread availability, however all four must be covered to be thorough. We will cover each in order presented above.

Loans and financial aid provided by colleges are a topic of great concern to many students, whether domestic or international. Many students, in my discussions, have told me that financial aid hindered their international colleagues from even applying to US schools. Although merit-based aid is often never granted at elite universities for anyone, need-based aid is almost always granted. First, we should speak on this point.

All selective private universities *will* provide students who are accepted the needed financial aid to attend college. If there is a demonstrated need, as it is called, it will be fulfilled by the university. Most private universities will fill demonstrated need, and they pride themselves on this fact. Colleges have selected you for your abilities and *want* you to attend their university, and will make that happen if finances are a problem. So in terms of applying, this should not be a concern. Apply because you feel the school is a fit and you can see yourself going there. If you see finances as a problem, it will be solved.

However, if there is not a demonstrated financial need and you fall under the merit category, but wish to cover your costs, there are a variety of options. At top-tier universities with low acceptance rates, merit scholarships are rarely if ever available. Consider that students accepted to top universities are already bright, how will they further differentiate and decide who should get scholarships? In the past, merit-based scholarships have been given out, but that is becoming less and less common. It may still be possible for extremely exceptional students to gain merit scholarships, although I have not heard of any instances. Athletes usually gain financial support, at any level of university they apply to.

If students apply to a liberal arts college, even very selective ones, with an emphasis on an area that is not so widely acknowledged, such as science, they may also get a merit scholarship. It is possible to get merit scholarships because these schools want to entice students with more diverse academic interests to their college. Some other private schools, such as USC, offer merit-based scholarships that require interview as well.

Loans

The most common route for students who do not have an obvious demonstrated financial need is that of loans. Even

for students in the USA, I have spoken to many financial aid offices and they continue to say that your family's income is the greatest determinant of financial aid availability.

In the United States, students complete the FASFA, Free Application for Federal Student Aid, and complete their CSS profile which must usually be completed at most colleges before consideration for aid. FASFA can be found

Perkins Loan

- A 5% interest rate loan intended for graduate and undergraduate students.
- Apply through school's Financial Aid office
- Borrow up to $5,500 for each undergraduate year and $8,000 for each graduate year

Federal Pell Grant

- You usually must be an undergraduate with no other degree, and the maximum award is $5,500 for one year (i.e. July 2009 to June 2010)
- Schools apply this grant to your school bill, and it is **need-based**

Federal Supplemental Educational Opportunity Grant (FSEOG)

- This grant is applied once eligible for the Federal Pell Grant AND with demonstrated financial need
- The amount can vary from $100 to $4,000 per year

Iraq and Afghanistan Service Grant

- This is a grant for those who do not demonstrate need but whose parent or guardian died due to military service after September 11, 2001 (this date may change in the future), with a maximum award of $5,500 per year (calendar year)

Teacher Education Assistance for College and Higher Education Grant (TEACH)

- For undergraduate, graduate, or postgraduate students taking or who will be taking the necessary courses to become elementary or secondary teachers, this grant requires that students attend a TEACH participating school

Direct Stafford Loan

- Subsidized Loans--inteded for undergraduate or graduate students with demonstrated financial need evaluated from the Free Application for Federal Student Aid (FASFA)
- Unsubsidized Loans-if you are not qualified for subsidized loans, usually because there is not a demonstrated need, students can ask for an unsubsizied loan. Payment of interest can take place while the student is still in school or choose to after they are out of school. In the second case, the total sum increases.

here: http://www.fafsa.ed.gov/ and CSS here: www.collegeboard.com/profile. These documents are often due in the beginning of February for incoming freshman. Some schools require W-2 forms and parent and student tax return forms as well, but these can usually be submitted after the FASFA and CSS. For California residents, students can apply for the Cal Grant at www.csac.ca.gov.

In the United States, federal loans are an option for students who are not fully covered financially. These fall under Federal Title IV loans, and are made up of:

Grants

Grants are financial aid that does not have to be repaid.

Work-Study

Work-study is an opportunity for students to work part-time jobs. Undergraduates get paid by the hour, usually in the range of $10 per hour, and will be paid directly and monthly by their school. These jobs are flexible and can work around academic schedules, and are usually on campus. Students can apply through their school's career center for these jobs. Often they are on-campus jobs that may require some training. Sometimes they are quite competitive to get.

Tax Savings

For US residents, federal tax savings can be collected as well by families of students, who are classified as **dependents**. There are four ways to collect savings:

American Opportunity Tax Credit	Tuition and Fees Tax Deduction	Student Loan Interest Deduction	Lifetime Learning Credit
• A $2,500 need-based tax credit maximum granted	• A maximum of $4,000 deductible from taxable income for parents jointly earning between $120,000 and $150,000. The deductible amount decreases as joint income increases	• A maximum of $2,500 deduction on interest paid for student loans	• A maximum of $2,000 tax credit per year for each **dependent**, with no limit for number of years of credit

Information from www.irs.gov/publications/p970

SCHOLARSHIPS

There are many, many scholarships for seniors. The two years to apply for scholarships in particular are 8th grade and 12th grade. In each of these years you are the top of the usual categories, middle and high school. These scholarships often fund parts of your college expenses and are generously donated by members of the community. There are few approaches to scholarships:

1. **Shotgun-local method**: In this method, you apply to many local scholarships ranging in value anywhere from $5 to $2,000 sponsored by local organizations or local branches of national organizations. If you decide to use this method, I would recommend applying to many scholarships. It will mean more work, but for the dollar value to be significant enough for the work you put in, I think that you should try to win more of these scholarships.

2. **Target-national method**: In this approach, you apply to fewer statewide or national scholarships that are usually prestigious and more competitive. Their dollar values range anywhere from several hundred dollars to many thousand dollars. I would work very hard on each application and try to be unique in each application because of the number of applications each of these scholarships requires. This approach should take less time than the **shotgun-local method** even if you spend quality time on each application. If you have a

"big thing" try to incorporate into your application for nationally-acclaimed competitions. This fusion usually works well.

Often, these scholarship deadlines are close to those of college applications and you must decide which to pursue. That is why I have given scholarships individual attention. Part of the application process is about time management, one of the topics discussed in the first chapter of this work. How you organize yourself will be very important in how many applications you can do successfully and how well you feel you convey yourself. Organization also becomes key in developing your presentation.

I would recommend the **target-national method**, especially for students who have a developed **"big thing"**. Every successful applicant has a **theme** in their application, and that should also shine through in your scholarship essays. Therefore, the question is again about time management — how well developed is your theme and can you easily write it, following your **one-sentence approach**, in scholarship essays. I recommend this strategy to all students, as well, because it seems to overall take less time than the other approach. If you are to undertake the first approach, make sure that you apply to most of the opportunities you get word of. That is the only way that this approach is effective and the time that you spend on doing scholarship essays instead of college essays is worth it. Because of this, applying via the second method can result in more scholarship money, more time on your essays, and more preparation time for the entire process.

From my own experiences and from the experiences of my peers, I have found that this is indeed true.. Do not worry about your competition, focus on what you can change: the quality of your application. Just a word of warning though: nationally-recognized scholarships are prestigious because they are *hard* to get. The time you spend on them could end up being greater than applying to a fewer, *easier* to get scholarships. Also remember that admissions officers can gauge the relative prestigious and corresponding difficulty of scholarships: gaining one very prestigious scholarship usually means more than five local, unheard of scholarships.

See the next page for a cycle of productivity and improvement that exists between students and parents.

Parents	Students
Find scholarships from magazines (subscribe to Johns Hopkins CTY magazine and similar)	Select which scholarships they like and try them
Encourage them to do activities	Students eventually like writing or winning scholarships and get motivated
Drive them there and watch for "seed passions"	Ask for more scholarships

THE RECRUIT

There are a few different types of recruits. The most common is the sports recruit. You will know if you are a recruit, especially if you are aiming for this niche for admissions to top colleges. Preparation is key for any chance at these kinds of institutions, and you will have been preparing for a long time, just like those who fall in the academic niche. I was recruited to some schools for tennis, and spoke to many premier athletes about their experiences.

First, realize that you will be accepted for a combination of your academic skills, personality, fit with the school, and your athletic ability. You will be accepted especially because you have unusual athletic ability and coaches believe that you can represent their school at inter-school events and competitions. Prepare to spend time on your sport in college—it is your extracurricular activity and your theme, after all, it should be your passion. Prepare to spend a lot of time in college working on your skills. Many of my contemporaries who are also athletes in college wake up exceptionally early several days of the week to work out. They also have multi-hour practices every day or every other day.

First demonstrate your exceptional athletic ability. This is done by the competitions you have entered and perhaps won—including invitational competitions. Coaches love going to national competitions because they can scout many athletes at once, all at the same, or similar levels. Of course, to reach this stage you have to be very good. If you are borderline recruit, it is possible to include supplementary materials that augment you strengths in your particular sport, although often times coaches will ask you to try and **walk-on**, or try out if you get accepted not as an athlete. For some sports, recruiting videos can be made to demonstrate specific talents.

Athletes can start contacting coaches of specific schools they really want to attend whenever they want. Update them about tournaments you have won or are participating in and maintain a line of communication, just like you do with faculty members when demonstrating interest in specific colleges. Some athletes have contacted coaches starting in sophomore year even. However, if you are top level recruit, be upfront with coaches and let them know if you are not intending on going to that school. Coaches have many possible recruits and want you to be clear about your intentions. Coaches currently are not allowed to contact you officially before 11th grade and at most once a week, but athletes can call coaches as many times as they want to. Sometimes athletes can apply earlier to colleges than regular or even early action or early decision candidates.

Coaches at many institutions, and in particular Ivy League schools, use the Academic Index (see "The Academic Index") to determine if a possible recruit could make the admissions cut academically. Some experienced coaches are able to tell from just looking at your transcript if you have a chance at these kinds of schools.

In your applications, the key is not to be one-dimensional. After you think you have demonstrated solid athletic talent, make sure that you demonstrate your intellectual passions or anything else you have a passion for (community service, for example). The key to admissions for athletes is to demonstrate a multi-faceted nature *along* with exceptional athletic ability. This athlete niche requires just as much work as the academic niche but you devote your time to other activities.

You could invite coaches to your competitions, although they will already be attending the major ones in your sport. Be yourself when you know they are scouting. This is the key — relax before these events more so than usual and just perform like it was a regular game.

LIKELY LETTERS

Some students, very few, receive likely letters. These letters are usually sent by top universities who are athletically recruiting students. Often, they suggest that you are going on the "right" path and that your application looks "strong". Usually they do not mention acceptance. There are a small group, very small, who receive academic likely letters. I think these students have been recommended by someone inside the university who has been impressed by supplementary work or by the application to an extent that they want to make special note to you.

I was fortunate to receive a likely letter to an Ivy League school for the academic niche. It came via email, as it does for most universities. Within a few days, it came by mail. If you receive a likely letter, you will know.

This is how I approached it: Ok, Ishan, I have got a likely letter. That means that I had a **"hit"** with an admissions officer or someone at that university. It also means that I have approached the process correctly, at least for this university. I will continue working how I have been and thinking how I have been. The letter does not explicitly state that I have been accepted, so I will not take it as so. Even if the *probability* is very high that I will be accepted, I will focus on what I can change.

If you receive this kind of letter, consider it assurance that what you are doing is right, but do not bank on it. I did not tell any of my peers that I received such a letter or even my teachers or counselor. For a while, I kept it to myself. After all, it was all based on hypotheticals: I was not accepted yet.

The likely letter should be motivation to work even harder in high school on everything that you do. It is recognition for you, assurance. So I focused harder and started working harder on everything that I did because I knew people acknowledged my work. Some student would think that "slacking off" would be practical now — since there is a high chance that you will be accepted. NO! At this point again, true passion and dedication is found.

THE FACULTY/DEAN RECOMMENDATION

There is a very small niche that deserves recognition here: the faculty or the dean recommendation. These students are recommended to attend a particular institution because of extraordinary talent that is noted by someone significant in the university. Often, the individual who recommends you will have close connections or easy access to the admissions office. You may or may not know that they are recommending you. Sometime you will know if you receive a likely letter or other times you will not receive any notification.

Sometimes, a very strong legacy connection or a large donation can result in recommendations. These are indirect ways of getting into college. For those students who do fall into this category, I still have recommendations. Read through the philosophies of embracing your work. You will need this at any step of your life. I recommend, especially for top schools, that you still develop your resume as if you did not have the niche. This way you hedge your bets: if you get in, it is because of *both* your merits and your recommendation. Although some may say that you got the "easy" way in, *you* will know that you also worked to get in. Knowing what it means to work will help you far more than admissions to any top school. I believe that every student admitted to every school is thoroughly inspected before being admitted, even with a recommendation. Grades, SAT/ACT, SAT Subject Tests, extracurricular activities, and a theme should be strong in any application. The difference between acceptance and rejection is the *level* of strength that each of these aspects is completed to. I recommend to every student to embrace the process and try his/her best because then your *level* will automatically increase.

For these students, a final word: disregard what others think about you — "Oh he is the one with legacy...that is why he got in". Focus on developing yourself, your resume, and you activities. In the future, past college, these skills will come in handy and eventually everyone will know why you were accepted. Make this reason because you were *good*. You just have a backup that others do not. Do not rely on it.

COLLEGE VISITS

There are two different ways of approaching college visits. Both are equally popular in my opinion, but I believe one is more logical and makes more sense than the other.

1. Visit potential colleges before being admitted.
    a. This could be before applying to get a sense of the University or after applying if it happens to be close and you want to judge the University if you get in.
    b. This could potentially give you a better sense of the University when you apply and when you write essays that deal with having an understanding of the University.
    c. If you plan on applying and also visiting many colleges, it will be costly.
    d. This plan is based on hypotheticals at its core.
2. Visit colleges after you are admitted.
    a. You might not get as good of a feel for the atmosphere of the University as if you had visited.
    b. You get to see your tangible choices before deciding. Every visit counts towards your decision.

I strongly espouse the second approach, visiting colleges after you are accepted. First, I think the first approach bets on hypotheticals and does usually cost money. There is an exception in which approach one should be taken: if you live close to the University, you can visit it to get a feel. But usually I think most of the universities you apply to may not be that close.

The second approach is based on reality. You have been admitted to certain institutions and *you* now have the power to accept them or not. You can fully judge them now and what better way than to visit the schools. Every visit counts because you visit the schools for which you have been given a seat.

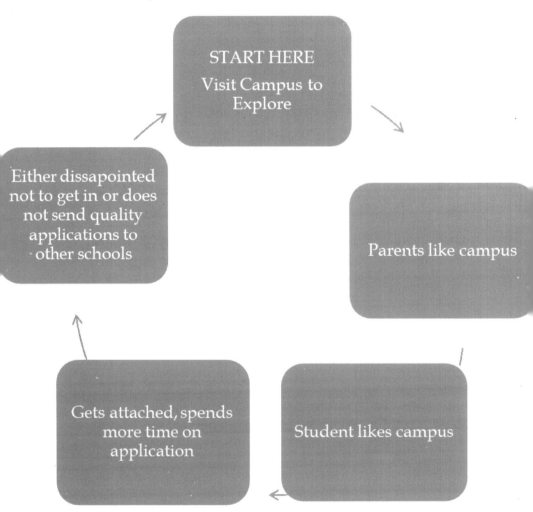

A GENERAL WORD ON COLLEGE VISITS

College visits usually entail a college tour. These tours are good for a general overview of a university and various facilities. Perhaps you learn some of the many facts that most of those tours offer. These tours do serve this critical function. However, often they do not convey completely student life on a particular campus or all the aspects of the school.

I suggest that if you visit a university, talk with students. They are just like you, except a few years older. If you choose students who do not seem to be in a rush, they will be happy to talk with you for a few moments. On my visits, I learned the most from my interactions with current students. They are usually laid back and will give you the true insight into particular courses, faculty members, or overall life. If you can really get a conversation going, try to ask them to see their dorm room. Tell them that the messiness does not matter.

Visiting the dorms and seeing the "real" dorms — not the ones that have been cleaned up — will help you truly realize the school atmosphere. I visited the dorms of a school where calculus equations were on the walls and in student's rooms. They did not tell me about this during the tour. I also visited another with ceilings that were lower than usual.

Perhaps if you know someone at the university you have applied to, try to arrange an overnight stay with them. College students are used to having visitors in their rooms and they will not hesitate to make room for you. I understand that overnight stays are offered by some colleges after acceptance — I HIGHLY recommend attending these stays. These stays helped me make my final decision.

INTERNATIONAL CASE STUDIES

To examine the "international" in practical, real-life terms, I asked classmates from Stanford, Harvard, University of Pennsylvania, and Columbia who applied from the many locations around the world if I could interview them, asking about their general experiences with the process, the myths, and how they fared. The information they gave me confirmed some of the notions about the process (such as its very competitive nature) that I gained from classmates at different universities. I suggest that you read the previous chapter "The International" before reading this case study.

It was a fairly cloudy day in the summer of 2009 when Shiv Parekh and I met. For London, the clouds were not unusual — actually it was fairly good weather, as the students attending Imperial College told me. Shiv and I were housed at Imperial College as part of the London International Youth Science, a two-week science conference where representatives from over fifty countries came to present their scientific research. We were both on the younger side at the conference — both 16 at the time. Since then, we have kept in contact and eventually reconnected as we found each other at Stanford University on a similar, but sunnier August summer day.

When I called Shiv to interview him, I first asked about his general impressions of the admissions process. He told me that he believes the notion that the admissions process is more competitive for international students applying to the United States than for students from the

US applying domestically. Though we cannot prove one way or the other, Shiv told me that at Stanford 7% of students in the undergraduate realm were internationals — a definite minority. 2010's admission rate of 7% overall must also be considered in this analysis.

Shiv went to school initially at a very good private school in Bombay, India. I actually know many students from that school, The Cathedral and John Connon School, from Harvard Summer School 2008 all the way to classmates in the Stanford Class of 2014, 2011, and 2010. Although I find that many student who come to US schools come from international schools, The Cathedral and John Connon School is a counterexample. At this school, Shiv says that students take AP tests if they are aiming to be admitted to US schools. For Gayon and Kemar, they went to school in Jamaica and the "public" and "private" school system was not necessarily existent. Instead, they have a sort of hybrid school structure: they went to a great public school that was also supported privately partially. They tell me that about 10% of their classmates applied to US schools — and these were the top students. Of them, very, very few were admitted. In particular, they told me that the process was *extremely competitive*. From their experiences, getting the necessary financial aid to make the education possible was the major factor. Although some students received admission, many did not get the necessary aid to attend. They say that they are proud and feel a little lucky to be here today.

Shiv then went to Sevenoaks School in the UK, which was a premier international school. He approximates that about 10 percent of his class took the IB curriculum in hopes of coming to the US for college studies. He estimates that in other UK schools, including non-international schools, that the percentage of students applying internationally and to the US is much, much lower (he estimates about 2 percent). For Shiv, he found that the SAT centers were far off (at least one hour away from his residence) and that much of the preparation he did on his own. I can verify that many of my international friends (specifically one from South Korea, one from Taipei, and one from India) did much of their standardized testing preparation independently. If you are an international preparing to apply internationally, remember that this may be the reality for you and you must prepare to take the exam, in terms of material and also logistics (sign up to take these exams earlier so you know where and when you can take them).

Through my own perspective and through many international students, as they tell me directly, most students who come to the US or go internationally for school tend to go to elite secondary schools. Although this does not have to be the case, and I can think of several counterexamples, the majority tend to go to elite schools that in some way prepares students for the application process — at that most students said their preparation entailed only knowing what to do, like take the SAT or ACT, and not actually the practical aspect of doing that.

Shiv said that the *BIGGEST* flaw in international students' applications to the US and other international schools was the lack of extracurricular activities. If you are an international student reading this, know that in the US extracurricular aspects and a "rounded" individual are highly prized and respected. Shiv said that the lack of the respect for "roundedness" in the UK may be a result of the admissions process there, which emphasized subject-based knowledge, final declaration of major during the admission process that also determines prestige of your degree, and the interviews for college admissions which were also subject-based. Still also know that sometimes the degree of your extracurricular activities, even if you conduct them, may not be enough. The truth of the matter is you really never have a "safe" amount of extracurricular involvement. Just know that if you tried your best, utilized your time to the fullest, and were also successful in studies, then you are probably fine. For my Stanford friends from Jamaica, Gayon and Kemar, their school mandated that they be involved in a sport, in a club, and so forth. However, as they tell me, even this is not enough: the process ended up rejecting most of their fellow classmates. You must try and do an extracurricular that you *truly love* because then you will spend time doing it, you will become good at it, and you will stand out. That is what college admissions officers are looking for.

For the practical aspects of applying, such as developing a theme and knowing the importance of extracurricular activities, Shiv said that he did a lot of independent research. Every single other case study agreed with Shiv on this: most of the research about practicalities is done *independently.* For me, this was also true because I wanted to gain a deeper (even historical) understanding of the process that began to consume so much of my time. Mostly he did online research, but probably also consulted some friends who had gone through the process. Two other case studies, two of my Stanford classmates both from Jamaica, Gayon and Kemar, also pointed out that a significant amount of understanding was gained from older classmates who were applying. Kemar, for instance, learned about the SAT examination from older classmates. For internationals applying, I hope that this book will help close that gap and also let you know on which elements to place importance on and which to leave until the end. Again, I stress the importance of your own research on sites like College Discussion—I gained much of my insight and formed many of my opinions based on data on these sites.

Shiv also said that many of his classmates who applied internationally actually did not get admitted and stayed in the UK or Europe for education. Kemar and Gayon reflected this same notion: many of the students who applied did not gain admission to US schools. This fact shows both the very competitive nature of internationals applying to the US and the lack of information that internationals have about the US application process. I stress international students to read this entire book because the above part applies to you as well as to the domestic student—developing a theme is key because it demonstrates vision, drive, and a sense of self and purpose. The discipline of this theme is not as important, as long as it is done at a certain level or with certain recognition within the community.

TO THE COUNSELOR

I have always admired counselors and facilitators because in my opinion you are faced with one of the hardest jobs in the world: balancing advice with letting the student become his/her own. This fine balance is only achieved if great care, wisdom, and experience combines with a passionate individual who wants to give back to the community.

Many of the previous aspects of the SAT/ACT, SAT subject tests, and extracurricular activities should give you a sense of what admissions officers are *roughly* looking for.

There is no formula to getting accepted to college, even for state schools or schools that seem like "safeties".

There is no such thing as "getting in" to colleges, it is called "acceptance" because it is a thorough process that is not a system that can be worked to perfection. At the same time, it is a pseudo-game that has rules and general "recommended" guidelines or features that are very desirable.

One of the other advantages of this book, especially to the counselor, is the mindset that I put forth. I have been very grateful and lucky to have *wonderful* counselors, and they mirror many aspects of my philosophy. The high school years and the application process are both experiences that shape the individual and not just necessary precursors to some occupation. They are an opportunity to find passion. I think that a successful counselor recognizes this and the individuality of the process for every student. The goal is try and inspire the student through this philosophy to grow on his/her own in whatever way they see fit. Pushing the student should (in the best of circumstances) turn into **self-drive**. I know this is idealistic and not possible for every student, but I think it should be the goal with every student.

For me, the counselor was the first one to introduce me to the academic world that college admissions look at. Mr. Randy McLelland gave me brochures about the SAT, ACT, subject tests, and AP tests that helped to orient me in this totally new world. I think this is one of the key roles of the counselor: to present opportunities and educate the student community on the basics of the academic *and* personal aspects that college admission officers look at. In addition, in the junior and senior years, the counselors were key to introducing us to the other aspects that admissions officers look at: essays and the interview. Remember, because I know that counselors often have hundreds of students to serve, the goal is to give a basic understanding and perhaps inspire students to investigate themselves further. For those students who become motivated, counselors should also have a deeper knowledge of the process to serve those students.

This deeper knowledge was critical for pushing me to doing my own investigation and pushing me even further. I often researched for hours on different elements of the process and developed some specific questions like: would west coast schools prefer the SAT or ACT? Understand that with the power of the Internet, many of these questions can be self-answered. Actually, most of my deeper impressions of the process came from personal investigation and from asking peers of their experiences.

As a counselor, I encourage something rather unorthodox, but very effective: search blogs, especially CollegeConfidential. Learn. That is what I did for thousands of hours over the course of four years and the knowledge of others really helped to form some of my opinions on the entire process. Maybe more importantly, I saw students portfolios (their grades, scores, essays) and then their results. There were historical records of what happened, and history tends to repeat itself. Being technologically linked in this way is something that I think should be a first priority for counselors. I think I gained years of experience and insight because others on the Internet were willing to tell their story. This is perhaps one of the most valuable sources I personally had, and I think if counselors have this knowledge and combine it with real-world experience and connections, they become very, very valuable sources. This would be my ideal counselor.

If I were a counselor, I would hold educational fairs and sessions with groups of students or, preferably, with the entire class, that outlines the whole admissions process and the necessary knowledge at each step of the high school experience. For example, for entering freshman I would have an information session that talks about choosing high school classes, choosing which clubs to join, and so forth. For juniors just beginning their academic year, I would hold a session discussing the essays for applications to colleges and asking for letters of recommendation at the end of the year or the beginning of senior year.

Another idea for counselors is to work in groups amongst themselves. Although in a sense counselors from different schools may be "competing" for spots at the same school, I think collaboration is essential to broadening understanding by combining perspectives. I personally believe counselors from the same area should meet once a semester or so to discuss the whole process and their perspectives. If there are national conferences for educators, I think counselors in particular should attend some of these. Awareness is key not only for students but also for counselors.

Finally, I propose another unorthodox measure: although there should be some distance between counselor and student, I think that students need to feel comfortable with counselors. Counselors and students should both make attempts to know each other personally. I find that this personal relationship usually grows out of the time that counselor and student spend working on academic schedules, discussing which schools to apply to, which classes to take, interviews, essays, and the entire process. It is important to point out that counselors are aware of the benefit of a closer relationship. It helps them when writing letters and makes both the student's work and the counselor's job fun and more effective. At least for me, I felt that I could tell my counselor what I honestly felt about the process and specific elements of the process because I had gotten close with him after years of working with him. Especially when college admissions come in, students often become emotional because they invest themselves in the process and counselors sometimes are an integral crutch for students. They led them and were key in the entire process. Knowing that someone has more experience and knows the entire application was comforting, at least for me.

ON THE PRIVATE COUNSELOR

There is much controversy, especially among parents who want their sons and daughters to attend very competitive colleges, on the efficacy of the private counselor. To be honest, the college admissions process is an *individual* process—between the admissions officers and the student, a dialogue and a story. That is why I have emphasized the perspective of the applicant because I know that personally and often speak about the admission officer and his/her perspective. At the end of the day, no matter what was done in the interim, it is a very *unique* process for every individual.

That being said, private counselors can be very useful if they have insight and experience beyond yours, which is often the case, especially with good counselors. If your school counselor has taken the steps I have mentioned above or is very established in the academic community, then a private counselor may not be necessary. Even if your school counselor is not like I have described above, it is still possible to gain that experience and insight through thousands of hours of surfing the Internet reading College Discussion and other academic boards. That is what I did.

I know some private counselors and even have had interactions with some of them. They did point out interesting opportunities and are useful if you do not want to devote those hours surfing the Internet and soaking in the information for yourself. I did spend these hours, and much of what they were telling me was reiterated by these boards or by direct conclusions I could draw. It all comes down to this: are you willing to spend many hours reading boards and through the Internet or do you want the information now and in less time?

After all, if I have found something integral to the admissions process it is the **value of information**. Knowing when and where something is happening can be quantified and is valuable. Because private counselors are supposed to know these things, they can provide information about events in your area or in other areas. This information can be found by anyone on the Internet, but bringing it together takes time. This is where the private counselor can help.

In addition, if you happen to know a "superstar" private counselor who has had years and years of experience, perhaps in the admissions office as well, then they have connections and insight that might not be on the Internet. I know some of these "superstar" counselors — they do exist. Again though, they are not necessary to gain

---

THE PRIVATE COUNSELOR MYTH

Sometimes some parents and students think that a private counselor is necessary for gaining admission to colleges, especially very competitive institutions. THIS IS NOT TRUE.

Thankfully, with the invention of the Internet and sites like College Discussion, much of the experience and insight that can be gained from a counselor can be scoured by the individual. I will admit I spent thousands of hours on these sites, but if you are not willing to do this then a counselor becomes very valuable.

Still, at the end of the day, the admissions process is an individual process between applicant and admissions officer — not between anyone else. There is no need for a private counselor, but they can sometimes be very helpful.

---

admission to top universities or universities at all — this is where another myth comes in, that can be both costly to parents and frustrating to students.

I do not want to say that private counselors are worthless — in many cases they can be very, very useful. If you do not want to devote hundreds and hundreds of hours investigating the process through online discussions, discussions with successful previous applicants, and with your school counselor, then private counselors will definitely be beneficial. But if you have that drive and motivation and truly enjoy the process, then perhaps you can gain that experience and insight through your own investigations. I am a big believer in autodidactic learning—teaching yourself. Another special case is if you know a superstar private counselor who can offer advice and connections that cannot be found on the Internet.

But I honestly believe that the hype about private counselors—especially among worried parents—is too much. I believe that they are not as necessary as parents especially make them seem. You can do it on your own if you want to. If you want another perspective, insight, and real-world experience, then yes, counselors can be very useful. All I want to say here is that private counselors are not necessary for admission—because the process is between the applicant and the admission officer. The counselor informs the applicant and makes him/her more knowledgeable about the process and about opportunities that can turn into the **"big thing"** or a significant extracurricular activity.

PART 4: ACADEMICS

COURSE LOAD SELECTION

Your course load selection becomes very important in the application process as trends are created. First I will write a little on misconceptions regarding the Advanced Placement and International Baccalaureate programs. From the results of my contemporaries, I have found that both programs are equally accepted by admissions officers. Whatever you school offers, take that without worry. If it does not offer either of these, also do not worry. I was at a meeting with a Harvard University admissions officer and a student from a rural school with no Advanced Placement examinations asked if he would be at a disadvantage. Indeed, if your school does not offer these exams you must still prove yourself. Finding nearby schools to take these exams at — or perhaps even farther schools — will be a story in itself and show your dedication and how you overcame difficulty.

I think that your selection in the number of AP/IB tests to take should be affected by a number of factors:

1. High caliber schools. If you are thinking of applying to top schools and want to increase the chances of getting in, you really have to take most or all of your school's AP or IB classes. No exception really., although you do not have to take all of them necessarily. Taking most of the difficult classes is the most guaranteed way of demonstrating commitment.
2. Your passions. If you have a particular area of interest, say physics, then definitely take the AP/IB

of this course, even you are not aiming to apply to schools with exceptionally low acceptance rates.

3. Conflicts with other large activities and competitions. There are some nationally-recognized events that directly conflict with the AP/IB test administration. Make sure that if this does happen to you, that you have a backup plan. I believe that both test services offer make-up exams — which also have the reputation of being more difficult.

In the application process, you want to demonstrate passion, vision, and dedication to admission officers. AP and IB tests are one standard and accepted way to do this. It shows academic willingness to challenge yourself. I am sure many admissions officers have taken these exams for themselves and know the difficulty and the preparation required. If you are in the academic niche, you will assuredly need to take these exams because you are marketing yourself for you academic skills. Even if you are in another niche (legacy or athlete) you will need to take these courses for serious consideration to very elite schools.

Think about the perspective of the admissions officer. He gets two applications. Let us say both have the same SAT score, the same subject test scores, and GPA. Both are also interested in the same extracurricular: medicine. One has taken 15 AP tests and the other 3. Most likely the admissions officer will say that the student with 15 APs has challenged himself/herself more and probably accept this student. That said, from my experiences, there are thresholds in AP exams as well. If you take almost all AP classes, say 14, and another student takes all of them, say 15, I would postulate that there is not a significant difference perceived by admissions officers.

THE AP TEST MYTH

"Oh, you took all the AP tests, all 17 of them! I took only 16. You are going to be accepted to every college and I am going to be rejected because of that."

I know many parents and some students who believe this myth. Again, this is a FALSE myth. I believe in the admissions process there are thresholds. If you take say 1-5 APs/IBs you have challenged yourself and perhaps taken those classes that you truly enjoy. If you take say 5-10 APs/IBs you are doing all of those that you think you can or not taking the ones you dislike a lot. If you take anywhere from 10-20 APs/IBs you are taking most or all of the AP tests that fit into your schedule.

There is a difference between taking 10 and 17 exams, but I do not think a difference of 1 or 2 (at most) exams will make a significant difference.

That said, I think that every student can get score very well on any exam they *embrace*. It is the same idea. If you are aiming for schools with low acceptance rates, I would recommend taking every AP/IB that you can. It is the mentality that matters in my opinion. You truly see which students have that vision at the end of senior year. Many students, having acceptances in hand, drop AP/IB exams. This is a practical choice. But I think the mentality matters more than the short-term enjoyment one gets. Go for it!

THE ACADEMIC INDEX

The Academic Index is one of the ways which some colleges (in particular, Ivy League institutions and perhaps similar level institutions) gauge one of the Applicant Aspects, namely, Academic Capability. The Academic Index is usually used for college-level athletic recruits, to determine if they meet academic level of the university in general. The Index is a numeric value that differs between schools (some schools use a score of 5 others 9 and others a different value) that gets assigned to students in the application process. Remember, this value is calculated solely from those measures that are used in the process to "define" your academics: namely GPA, SAT/ACT, SAT subject tests, and sometimes class rank (which could be substituted for GPA).

There is a surprising aspect of the Academic Index—namely the weight that SAT Subject Tests are given. I personally did not truly realize the value that these are given until I saw the results of my contemporaries and my friends across several universities. Often, the combined score of their SAT Subject Tests was much higher than their composite SAT score or right on par if their SAT score was very high. At the same time, admissions officers have told me that SAT scores, whether SAT I or SAT II, are one day, sit-down exams that are not truly reflective of an individual's academic ability. They tend to stress cumulative GPA as more of an indicator, and I have found that most students tend to have very high GPAs.

The SAT Subject Test is more content-focused, as stated by a few studies done by the SAT and from my experiences. Admissions officers realize this and probably feel that they are more representative of in class academics. These exams offer a snapshot into the Academic Capability of the student at one particular time so that other factors — such as perseverance in classes, lack of sleep (which could affect GPA in a few classes), and outside stresses — can be eliminated. GPA is representative of total performance, perhaps, and SAT Subject Test results of true knowledge at a particular point.

Remember that the Academic Index is just a rough indicator. Do not get stuck to those calculators and worry about one student who has an AI score that is one or two points above yours. There are several other aspects of the applicant that the admissions officers look at. You should calculate your score out of curiosity, and compare these to the ranges that some sites offer for certain kinds of schools. Still, I would not get bound by these scores even when comparing them to these relative ranges. You can use your AI score in estimating the color of the school for the **red-yellow-green method** for choosing which schools to apply to.

Calculating the Academic Index

In the 1980s, the Ivy League implemented a tool called the Academic Index to gauge the basic academic credentials of recruited athletes compared with the student body over all. The tool calculates combinations of grade-point averages (G.P.A.) and scores from SAT, SAT II and ACT exams. Universities have their own requirements on which combinations they will accept. Below are a couple of options for calculating the index. It is not a way to determine admission since multiple factors go into that decision.

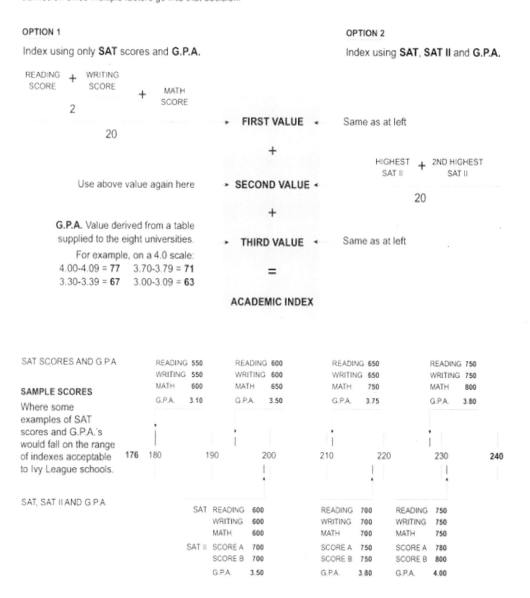

OPTION 1

Index using only **SAT** scores and **G.P.A.**

$$\frac{\dfrac{\text{READING SCORE} + \text{WRITING SCORE}}{2} + \text{MATH SCORE}}{20}$$

→ **FIRST VALUE** ←

+

Use above value again here   → **SECOND VALUE** ←

+

G.P.A. Value derived from a table supplied to the eight universities.
For example, on a 4.0 scale:
4.00-4.09 = 77   3.70-3.79 = 71
3.30-3.39 = 67   3.00-3.09 = 63

→ **THIRD VALUE** ←

=

ACADEMIC INDEX

OPTION 2

Index using **SAT**, **SAT II** and **G.P.A.**

Same as at left

$$\frac{\text{HIGHEST SAT II} + \text{2ND HIGHEST SAT II}}{20}$$

Same as at left

SAT SCORES AND G P A

SAMPLE SCORES
Where some examples of SAT scores and G.P.A.'s would fall on the range of indexes acceptable to Ivy League schools.

	READING	550
	WRITING	550
	MATH	600
	G.P.A.	3.10

	READING	600
	WRITING	600
	MATH	650
	G.P.A.	3.50

	READING	650
	WRITING	650
	MATH	750
	G.P.A.	3.75

	READING	750
	WRITING	750
	MATH	800
	G.P.A.	3.80

176   180   190   200   210   220   230   **240**

SAT, SAT II AND G P A

SAT   READING   600
      WRITING   600
      MATH   600
SAT II SCORE A 700
      SCORE B   700
      G.P.A.   3.50

READING   700
WRITING   700
MATH   700
SCORE A   750
SCORE B   750
G.P.A.   3.80

READING   750
WRITING   750
MATH   750
SCORE A   780
SCORE B   800
G.P.A.   4.00

AP AND IB TESTS

The Advanced Placement (AP) and International Baccalaureate (IB) examinations are an important way of demonstrating your academic and subject-specific strengths to colleges. By taking classes with these denotations, you get prepared to take near end-year examinations in those subjects, which are graded against other students who take the exams, for both AP and IB, across the world.

Some schools offer both AP and IB, and students often wonder which path to take. From my experiences and from talking to admissions counselors I have found that either is fine. Universities seem to have no preference, as long as you do the best you can in whatever you choose and take a strenuous workload. At a recent workshop I went to at Harvard University, one student asked if he would be at a disadvantage because his school does not offer AP or IB. The admissions officer responded, "No" and went on to explain that they are looking for students who do the most with what resources are available.

I have spoken to a few admissions counselors and they stress the importance of taking these exams and classes if they are offered at your school. There are hundreds of thousands of students who take these exams, and they demonstrate ability in particular subjects, like AP Calculus or AP English Language, that is a positive and definite strength. One counselor even said that these exams are more important or as important as SAT Subject

Tests. I would tell the student to focus on one step at a time, and to try your best at each of these academic tests.

AP and IB tests are critical to show admissions counselors your willingness to push yourself in hard classes, your ability in subjects, and your drive. Often students applying to Ivy League schools or equivalents take all or most of these classes at their school. If you are aiming for top schools, I would recommend the same. Consider it from the admissions officer's perspective: he gets two applications, one with a student who has taken all APs offered and one who has not. If their GPAs are similar, or even if the first student is a little lower than the second, almost always the first will get a higher mark on the academic side. That being said, if you are truly unable to take a particular subject, do not fail out of the class because you need another AP or IB class. But still, in my experiences and through the experiences of all of my classmates, these classes are manageable if you put hard work into them.

THE STANDARDIZED TESTS

The SAT Reasoning Test and the ACT are two of the most commonly accepted standardized tests among colleges. In my experiences, they are critical to your acceptance and tell more than just a single numeric score to admissions officers, which is why they place so much emphasis on them. I will detail a general plan, my personal approach, and the reasons why I think these tests are important and are necessary.

But for the majority of students, including me, we cannot bank on this approach. It is a myth, in my opinion.

THE ONE-TEST WONDER MYTH

We have all heard the myth about that student who did not take any practice tests, walked in on exam day, and got a 2400. I have never met such an individual. But even if he/she does exist, there are a few reasons why it is possible:

1. He/she thinks EXACTLY like the exam writers (highly unlikely)
2. His/her math skills, writing skills, and reading skills were matched particularly to that exam
3. He/she frankly got lucky

I think that this combination of prerequisites is almost impossible. I do not want to say impossible because there is always a statistical chance that any thinking being can take the test and mark every answer correctly without even reading the questions. But do not assume that you are not him/her. Even if you are, does hard work ever come to waste? Do not assume, just work.

There is frankly only one way to master the test and that is through hard work, vision, and a detail-oriented, progressive approach. I believe that for most people there is one way to master these exams: take tests. Over and over. But the key is to *learn* from your mistakes and not just mindlessly take exams. The philosophy of *embracing* the process is KEY here. It really is, in my opinion and from what I have seen.

Now for some thoughts on getting tutoring for the SAT or ACT. Any student can benefit from any sort of tutoring. Tutoring can never really hurt unless the student decides to go against the system. But I think once again the key is to first *embrace* the exam. Without this embracement, no amount of cajoling, tutoring, or encouragement will do much.

Once the student has accepted the exam as a major part of their life and is ready to devote themselves to the exam, he/she should decide for himself/herself if they should get tutoring.

STUDENTS: In the case of tutoring for these nationally-recognized exams, do not think that it is like regular tutoring. I had never got tutored, but I needed it for the SAT. I consider it *training*, not tutoring. Do not be ashamed to do it, because these exams are very specific and ask you to think in specific ways.

Students should get tutoring if they want a more well-defined way of approaching the test. If they want to have some pre-defined ways of thinking (especially for the writing portion of the SAT), then tutoring will benefit them. The key here is to thoroughly understand the material in the readings that various companies disseminate and the strategies they encourage — especially time management strategies.

However, I strongly believe that every student develops his/her own way of approaching the test and eventually his/her own strategies for individual questions, sections, and passages. This approach, if the student goes to training (as I will call it), will be a hybrid of the strategies that the test preparation company gives and the students interpretation of these strategies. This hybrid is what I eventually discovered of myself after having taken several test preparation courses.

If the student studies individually, which is entirely possible and which actually gave me the final boost in my preparations, strategies will be entirely his/her own. Individual studies are recommended, in my opinion, for students with *great drive*, who can sit down every Saturday at 9 AM and study until 4 PM. These students are motivated more than 99% of students and usually do well in whatever they put themselves to.

For most students I encourage a mix of training and self-study. This mix is what actually turned out to be the best for me. I took the strategies I liked from test preparation companies and combined them with my own strategies that I made up after taking dozens and dozens of exams and reviewing where I went wrong. I was able to take the best of both approaches — I highly recommend this for any student. But again, motivation is key because studying on your own — especially for an exam in the far future—was difficult and required more effort than most things I have ever done.

A NOTE ON TEST PREPARATION COMPANIES

As we know, there are many test preparation companies. Many of the larger ones, such as Kaplan, Princeton Review, and Elite, offer test preparation classes that vary in length, intensity, and usually difficulty. In my experiences, I have found that smaller, individually run, test preparation companies are often the best. These are usually founded by one or two individuals who devote themselves to one of the two exams (SAT or ACT) and make their livelihood preparing students for the exam. I recommend these particular companies because:

1. Individual attention. If you are a motivated student, it will show by how much you truly care about every question you missed, even after 5 hours of taking tests. By asking questions, you can show your passion and the teacher will notice. You can get help for your specific problems more easily. Also, the teacher can get to know you better in these kinds of settings and in particular your weaknesses and strengths.

2. Often the teachers of these test preparation companies love what they do and *want* to help you. They have a love for teaching and an unusual skill for each particular exam. Many times, they are better teachers because they want to be there and because they enjoy the process. If they are very good instructors, they have *embraced* the exam and want you to as well.

3. It is sometimes easier to focus in settings where the atmosphere is not entirely structured and laid out beforehand. I have asked my friends who have taken courses at larger test preparation companies and they often say that sometimes it is hard to focus because of the regiment that they must follow.

There is an exception to this general philosophy, and that is when the student is short on time. If you are a senior and reading this book in early August, I would instead recommend taking a condensed course over Winter Break offered by some test preparation companies (such as Elite). You are short on time, and you need the preparation and as much as you can get. The more, the better, as long as you *embrace* the training and learn from it.

Here are the general steps I have personally found helpful:

1. Take diagnostic exams of the SAT and the ACT. **You only need to master one, but make sure you chose the right one for you**. This could entail taking 3-4 practice exams. Make sure that you take a slew that is representative — do not take exams only from one test preparation company, vary your choices based on the reviews and experiences of others. Consider the general and honest attitudes that the universities you are considering applying to have about each exam. I believe that most universities consider each equally, but make sure.

2. Embrace your exam of choice. If you want to do this exam correctly, it will be a major portion of

your high school experience and it will take time. Realize and accept this.

    a. For the first five months of my preparation for the SAT (my test of choice), I did not fully embrace it. I listened to the general audience and my peers: man, the SAT is so boring! I took their word and followed what they thought. After taking the exam and not doing satisfactory, I decided to embrace the exam. My results greatly improved.

3. Develop a strategy (time-based) on precisely how many exams you are going to take in how much time.

    a. At the beginning of my preparations, for about five months, I would practice by doing individual sections and taking breaks between sections. This approach was not for me, and I believe this is not the way to approach such an exam. Instead, *do the entire exam as if it were real with actual time constraints, every time.* This way, you will get used to the format, the material, and your own pace. At first, you may not feel comfortable at all, but eventually you will understand your own test-taking strategies and the test itself.

    b. Example: I will take one exam every week on Saturdays. I will start every Saturday at 9 AM and finish at 4 PM with a one hour lunch break. I will review my exam after my break.

4. Take practice tests from every test company you can find, starting with the most well-known companies. Read about each company's reputation among students (for example, Barron's is usually considered more comprehensive) and keep this in mind. If you are hoping to truly master the exam, you will need to perform well on most of these exams, regardless of test company. Do not worry, this success will come with the right preparation.

5. REVIEW. Review your exams, every single time, once you finish the tests. Do not wait until the next day because you will not remember your exact thinking process for every single question. If you do the test correctly and embrace every question, you will remember your thinking process for a few hours after the exam. REVIEW. REVIEW. REVIEW.

   a. The most common mistake for students is not to thoroughly review their exams. They take the test, and think they are finished. I did this for the first five months of preparation.

      i. What do I mean by review?

         1) During your first dozen exams, go over every single question, reading the explanations for every answer, **including the ones you marked correctly**.

         2) Read the sample responses for every essay prompt. Read your essay and look for a concrete thesis and other

factors that are specifically
targeted by SAT essay
readers. If you truly want to
master this essay, there are
several books and tutors that
target the essay.

Again, I want to re-emphasize reviewing your
exams. Without a thorough review, which could take half
as long as the actual exam, one really does not learn. Doing
the test over and over will result in great time
management, but not a thorough understanding of the
material. The first time I took the exam, I had taken
perhaps 12 practice tests, but I had not *embraced* the exam
and I had not understood myself, the exam, or my
mistakes.

ON PRACTICING

I have taken both the SAT and the ACT, although I
specialized in the SAT. I have found with both exams,
however, that **consistent practice** is necessary. This phrase
means taking entire tests, in simulated settings, once a
week until the week of your actual exam. I know this
schedule will, in reality, take one full day of your week,
but it is necessary in order to do well. At least it was for
me and for most of the people I know who did well.

The first time I took the SAT, I did not take a full
test for one entire month before the actual exam. I did
practice on individual sections, but did not practice my
time management or format understanding. I believe that I

did unsatisfactorily mostly because I did not take enough simulated exams and did not practice consistently.

With **consistent practice** comes **constant focus**. We spoke on this term earlier in terms of general time management and success in high school. Now, **constant focus** is used on either the SAT or ACT. You will develop this focus if you take full-length exams. I realized my **constant focus** on my third attempt at the SAT. After finishing two sections of the exam, sitting in the hallway, I realized that I did not hear one sound around me when I was taking the first two sections. I was 100% focused on the exam. Nothing disturbed me for 50 minutes. If I had consciously attempted to gain this focus, I may have been able to further develop it before the exam. This focus means that you are able to take the exam through anything (rain, car horns, ambulances — all of which are possible on exam day).

A FINAL WORD

In my opinion, the SAT and the ACT are one of the most significant experiences you will have in high school. Looking back now, many students in college say how *insignificant* they all were. True, I also believe that it is not absolutely necessary to go to school to be successful, but for most of us, it is. These exams are significant, just like freshman year in high school. That is the honest truth.

I have covered the generalities of exam taking and what I have found is useful. But there is so much more, the specifics of each exam that you will need to learn from test preparation books, training, and from yourself as you take exams. This chapter could span most of the book if I attempted to detail these specifics. Read this chapter as an outline for what you are going to do, and for the attitude you are going to take in your endeavor. Do not worry if you do not ace the exam the first or even the second time. It is a learning process. At the same time, do not take each exam seven or eight times — you will assuredly be viewed negatively if you do this. College admissions officers are looking for individuals who tried their best and this is supposedly to appear on your score sheet. If you take the exam too many times (this exact number is for you to decide) they will see that exam taking is your *extracurricular*, something you definitely do not want to convey.

You develop a **personalized approach** to test taking, whether it be from your experiences with test preparation companies or by studying on your own. That is the end of the story: there is no magic pill to take or a quick success story. I found my personal approach after two years of preparation, from 10th to the beginning of 12th grade. I went to two tutors and combined their strategies to make my own. I also developed several strategies, especially for the critical reading portion of the exam, on my own.

For the SAT, I think the critical reading portion is the section that requires the most personalized approach. That is why, for many students, it is the hardest section to master. Having scored an 800 on this section, I found that it was a combination of **constant focus, constant practice,** and my own **personalized approach** that ultimately allowed me to achieve this score. I combined the reading of long passages from my first tutor with the reading of short passages and vocabulary from my second tutor and developed my own overall approach to critical reading sections. This is an excellent example of the kind of personalized approach I eventually found myself developing for the entire test. Ultimately, the way you think, your inclinations, and the way you understand the writing from test preparation books or the information from tutors will help to shape your approach. If you consciously are aware that you are making your own approach, the process will make more sense: do not believe the idea that one-size-fits-all, even for *standardized* test taking. Although they are standardized, the way you interpret them will be unique, and so your approach will be unique.

The development of this personalized approach could take two years, as it did for me, which is why I suggest that you start early but not make it an extracurricular activity. I know some students who started studying, by the pushing of overly worried parents, in the 7th grade. Although there is nothing wrong with early preparation, I only advise that there is time for the student to grow in other dimensions and freedom to do what he/she wants at times. This growth is vital to the development of a full human being, and in practice, is seen in the essays, the interview, and the overall admissions process. Finding this balance between starting early enough and giving time for growth is something that will be different for every individual again, which also makes it one of the hardest aspects of the entire admission process to gauge. Individualized attention is needed here, and perhaps this is where personalized tutoring would be useful. Please refer to the chapter titled: "On the Private Counselor" for more opinions, although those are related to the general college admissions officer and not the SAT tutor.

Be honest with yourself. Do not cheat yourself on practice examinations by inflating your score. Often, I gave myself the optimistic side and curve for practice SAT exams, and the first time I took it, I was very surprised by the lower-than-expected score that I received. If there is one thing I can stress about this process it is honesty. I take the approach of the **constructive realist**. Be constructive in your approach, and always know that these practice examinations that you are taking are for the better and are helping you improve. At the same time, be a realist. Know where you stand. But also believe that you can achieve the perfect score. Have that goal in mind at all times and know realistically how close or far you are from achieving it. This kind of paradox is found in many parts of application process: you must discover elements of the SAT and other standardized tests and become part of the "system" but you also must develop a personalized strategy to the test. You must be realistic about where you stand in test taking but also optimistic and honestly believe that you can score the perfect score with enough preparation. You must show potential and already have accomplished something. The process is quite paradoxical.

FOR TEST SPECIFICS:

Read College Discussion. This is perhaps *the* most beneficial online forum for all admissions related posts. But be very, very wary. The myths that are found throughout this book tend to spring up because misinformed or overly-concerned individuals propagate those myths on this website in particular. You need to read with a **critical eye**.

On College Discussion you will find many of the test specifics, like how to read SAT long passage sections (like circling key words that occur in each paragraph or first skimming questions then moving to answers or vice versa). I understand that in this book I have not really talked about these strategies and I consider doing so in future works. The purpose here is to give you perspective on the *entire* process and how to approach it. Read through the hundreds and hundreds of threads that exist on College Discussion with relation to test preparation and you will be adequately equipped to make your own **personalized approach**, which develops once you know these common methods and you apply your own thinking while taking practice examinations.

In addition, College Discussion can be useful for understanding some of the mentalities that exist about the process in general. You can freely read through those and through this book and combine them to make your own **personalized philosophy**. The key to the entire process is to make it your own, this book is a guide for you to know how to do that effectively.

SAT SUBJECT TESTS

SAT Subject Tests are important parts of the quantitative portion of the application. They serve to highlight your strengths in particular areas at a national level of competition. As I have seen, some admissions counselors suggest that they may be as important as the SAT or ACT itself. More and more, I am seeing the importance of these tests.

There are many approaches to these tests. First, and probably the most common approach, is to take the corresponding SAT Subject Test late in the school year during which you are taking that class. For instance, if you are taking AP Chemistry in your 11th grade, you would take the SAT Subject Test in June. Generally, I would agree with this approach, especially for content-heavy tests such as history, science, and perhaps math. However, for the language and English tests, I would say that this approach is not necessary.

There are number of factors to consider in this approach. First, another myth that is relevant to the SAT/ACT as well.

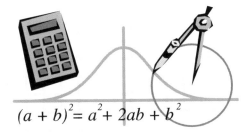

$$(a + b)^2 = a^2 + 2ab + b^2$$

THE CURVE MYTH

Many students have the opinion that certain months have "steeper curves" for exams, whether it be the ACT, SAT, or the SAT Subject Tests. Although this ends up being statistically true, I think your approach should not be significantly altered by such notions. This is especially true for those students aiming for prestigious schools. If you are aiming to do very well on the ACT, SAT, SAT Subject Test, or any other standardized test, the month in which you take it will not matter. I tried everything—I even took the SAT during the supposedly "easier" months twice—and it did not help. Instead, I scored the highest during one of the "steeper" months.

Do not believe in these myths. Focus on your own test-taking abilities and your progress. This approach is really the only way to be successful with the exam. You almost have to tunnel yourself into focusing on each exam, each question, and leave the hypothetical grade-grubbing to others. Success will come to those who can succeed at any time.

The number of SAT Subject Tests you should take is dependent on whether you took the SAT or ACT and other factors. Some schools require fewer SAT Subject Tests if you took the ACT and are planning on submitting this test. Others require the same number. Please consult the admissions page of your particular school to verify which approach it takes.

In any case, the number of SAT Subject Tests that you take should also be dependent on how many you have to submit. Most schools require you to submit two tests, but there are a number that require you to submit 3 tests.

I know some individuals who took seven subject tests. I also know individuals who took three tests and sent those three. I would recommend taking an intermediate number of tests and preparing very well for each one so that repeat exams are not necessary, if possible. This intermediate value is for you to determine, but I personally would take anywhere from 3-5 tests, including repeat tests.

There are further two approaches to which tests to take.

1. **Content-focused approach**: In this approach, you take exams around a particular subject area that you want to convey mastery to admissions officers. For example, take Math, Physics, and Chemistry and send the scores you receive from these tests. This would demonstrate mastery in the sciences and in mathematics. I have some friends who took this approach and were successful. I would recommend this approach if you know you have a knack for a particular area of study and you want to convey this throughout your application (your extracurricular focus and your theme also demonstrate excellence in a similar area). This approach is also good if you plan on pursuing a

field with those skills required. For example, taking all the science tests for entrance into a seven-year medical program or taking humanities tests for entrance into a liberal arts college.

2. **Diversity approach**: This approach is taken by most students. When you want to identify success in a number of fields and take exams across disciplines I would take this approach. I personally also took this approach because I did not have a defined focus for a professional career or a well-defined academic niche. Make sure that you study significantly for each exam, and also make sure to take the exams that your theme interacts well with.

THE SCORES

To be realistic with you, you will often need high scores in order to get into top tier universities. But at the same time, society inflates what you really would need. There is no cutoff, but there are plenty of students with 2100 SAT I at Stanford. A uniting factor is a high GPA, which is cumulative and established over time. Equally important to your grades are your essays, which is why I labeled an entire section of this work with focus on the essay. The idea of the SAT Subject Tests is to demonstrate excellence in particular areas. That is why I have stressed picking your subjects carefully, knowing which ones you will be able to excel in most.

SUPPLEMENTARY MATERIALS

Supplementary materials are often sent by successful applicants to many universities, but not always. These materials further demonstrate your theme and your niche. They allow you to communicate more clearly with the admissions officers and guide them in the direction you want them to view you in. However, once again, we need to be careful in the amount of material we send. Admissions officers have to review so many applications, and you want to give them just the right amount of material to understand you and not to be overburdened and desensitized to that which you send them.

So what are these "supplementary materials"? They can be optional supplementary **essays** or anything that demonstrates your **"big thing"** or your **theme** more clearly, such as a piano recording, called **out-of-application supplementary materials**. Schools will often ask for a supplementary optional essay in their supplement, and usually will mention what kinds of other materials, such as scientific papers or piano recordings, they accept. Often, they are quite particular about what they accept, but it truly depends on a schools-by-school basis. Some supplementary portions of applications give students an opportunity to submit an additional essay or additional comments. It is free space. We will start by analyzing this section.

Optional Essays

Yes, it is more work. Yes, it will require more thought and you should not repeat what you said in your essays. But it is also another chance to make your conversation with admissions officers more thorough! Therefore, I believe that every student, especially students applying to elite schools, should fill out this section if there is the option.

Here is how this section should be approached:

1. Sit at your desk, close your eyes for one minute, and clear your mind. Turn off Facebook, your cell phone, and any distractions. You are about to act as an admissions officer — they probably do not have music blasting in the background when they are reviewing applications.

2. Read your entire application, including the common application section, for this particular school. Read it as you think an admissions officer would. What perception do you get from your application? Is this what you want to convey? Additionally, what is the theme that you have conveyed and is this what you wanted to convey?

   a. This approach is valuable because it allows you to again review your essays and also look at the general attitude that you get from the conglomerate that is your essays and your entire application. It allows you to review your application for the meaning that you get from essays and from your overall application.

3. Now that you have fixed any discrepancies between your intended meanings and what you actually conveyed, focus on any additional details that you think you left out or were not conveyed very strongly. It could be a particular experience that could not fit as an example in your essays or it could be a general attitude or personality trait that is demonstrated by an activity that you really did not highlight. It really could be anything. Just make sure that it is not something strongly conveyed in your application.

4. Sit down and either start writing about the topic you feel you have not covered or alternately, if you prefer planning out your writing, jot your ideas in outline format in an electronic document.

5. Now that you have created some rough ideas and started honing in on the area you want to concentrate on, treat this segment like an essay. Consider the word count or character count that the entry has and write accordingly. This "open" entry should accurately convey something that is otherwise not conveyed.

I think that this "open" entry is another opportunity to differentiate yourself. Many students, especially those who procrastinate, may not have the time to do this portion of the application. Instantly, you demonstrate more care than these students. From those that have done this section, you will have edited it and put your heart into it — which will be visible. The best you can do is try your best and through this process you can work as much as you think will be your best. Time is the most valuable thing in this process.

This **time-centric approach** allows you enough time to write quality essays and a lot:

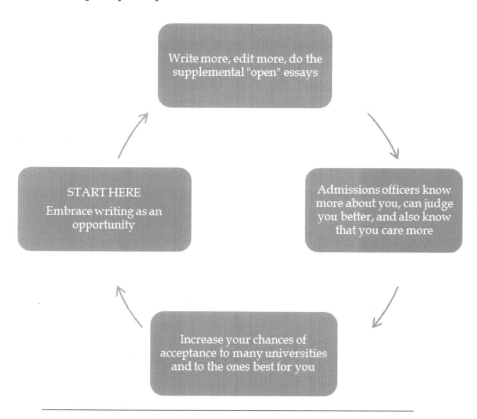

Scientific Papers/Recordings/Etc.

In addition to the "open" prompts that I consider supplementary materials, there are other **out-of-application supplementary materials** that some applications explicitly ask you to send and others that do not say anything about. These materials include recordings of music, science fair abstracts or entire papers, and artistic productions. These supplementary materials should be sent out around the time you submit your application and supplement, so colleges can link your Common App ID (which you should include in your additional supplementary materials) to your research or anything non-standard that you are submitting.

I would strongly encourage you to submit these kinds of material—ESPECIALLY for top schools. Anything that you can do to show how much you care and how much passion you have is always positive and necessary. Even if you are not applying to schools with exceptionally low acceptance rates, I would still send my supplementary materials. I sent supplementary materials to every college I applied to, whether it was asked for or not. I thought it contributed very nicely to my theme and conveyed my passion in an appropriate manner.

Before you send anything, think again on what you want to convey most to colleges. Think of your **one-sentence** that describe you and your theme. Think about your niche. Is there also any particular area that you have not articulated? I think that if the application does not have an "open" prompt this weakness—if it is significant to whom you are and your theme—should be included in your essays. The supplemental material you should send should be enunciating a strength evident in your application.

Examples:

1. Sending your research abstract that also won the California State Science Fair.
   a. If your theme is some sort of science research, then it should be evident in your essays. By sending your abstract, you can first prove that this is all legitimate and second *show*, instead of tell, your story and your research. It is always more poignant to read about something and then see it.
2. Sending the award-winning essay that was your entrance into the writing world.
   a. Again, this is *showing* the admissions officers your work.
3. Sending a musical composition or a copy of an art piece that won you recognition.

WARNING: These kinds of supplementary materials will be sent to faculty in that specific area, so they must be quality. Although faculty does not expect college-level research unless you say that, they do have a threshold for how good the work needs to be.

The examples listed are optimistic because they involve statewide, national, or international recognition. If you do not have this kind of recognition, do not worry. If you have ANYTHING, even local recognition, I would still send anything related to this success. Sending something denotes that you are proud of what you have done, that you have done it, and that you want to share your story with the admissions officers (which hints at a passion for the school and for the application process). Just be careful that it has to link to your theme and who you are as a flowing story — not a last-minute effort to send something extra in.

NOTIFICATION SUBMISSIONS

It has been perhaps one month since you have submitted your application and your supplementary materials. You may have also had your interview. You were, in the meantime, preparing for the large, internationally-acclaimed competition that occurred in January (for example, Intel Talent Search). You could not include this in your application because it had not occurred yet and you had not won any award.

But now that you have won this award or recognized an achievement, should you send the material to colleges? YES. YES. YES. Send these achievements with a cover letter explaining briefly what it is and what you won. You should identification information on this page that makes it very easy to match with your application. Also, use the same labels that you used to craft your completed application with supplementary materials.

THE PRESENTATION

The way you present your application, supplementary materials, and yourself at the interview should be cohesive and polished. A polished **presentation** — as I will call it — denotes organization, passion, confidence, and **self-drive**. Often, your **presentation** tells as much as your overall application.

So far, we have talked about the presentation of your application. That is, the cohesive way in which you weave a **theme** in all of your essays and the niche that you want to be placed in. We have talked about the necessity of sending supplementary materials. It is critical for applications to top schools and necessary, in my opinion, for applications to any schools that have acceptance rates less than 100 percent. It is a way to differentiate yourself — it is that "extra mile" that will show so many character qualities that you want to convey. We have talked about the interview, and how to prepare well for it by reviewing aspects about the school which you find interesting and by reviewing your **theme** in the written aspect of this process. Now it is time to talk about combining all of these aspects into the **presentation**.

The written work is viewed by admissions officers who never get the chance to meet you. They *want* to learn about you and have had many of the experiences you have had. I have stressed this part of the process so much because it is the admissions officers who ultimately decide if you get an acceptance letter or not.

Before beginning the process of printing out your supplementary materials (if needed), plan out how you are actually going to package your materials. Include your printed application to that particular school so that placement with you is easier. Organization is key in this part of the process.

First, print out labels with the "Application to X University" where you insert the name of the university. You will put these labels on top of each stack.

Second, print out labels with the schools addresses. Fill an entire page as it becomes complicated to print labels if some are already used although it is possible.

Third, print out labels with your own address and your name.

Now print out the entire application with essays and perhaps "open" prompts to each school. Organize these in different stacks.

Now print out your supplementary materials if necessary or make copies. Put these separately from all other piles. These are standardized, whereas some other piles are not.

Organize them as follows:

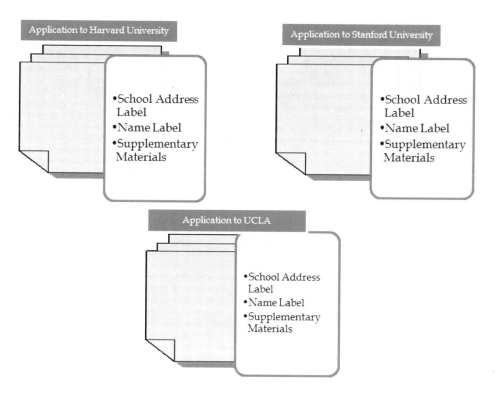

Because admissions officers get so many applications, it is necessary to focus them in on a theme. This should be conveyed throughout your application and furthermore through your supplementary materials. Your application should be submitted on time with all essays clearly polished and reviewed many, many times. The supplementary materials should be sent concurrently or a little later (not much later though). That way, admission officers can group your materials easily. Send your application in full and in hard copy along with your supplementary materials so that it is even easier to match your application with your supplementary materials. After all, much of the material you send by mail will be sorted in a systemized fashion. Make sure that you have all the addresses sorted out and create labels for each school. Print more than the number you think you need. You will need many, many labels if you are taking the **high-output approach**, which I encourage most often to students. Also create labels with your address, name, and any other information you feel necessary. This process can be very frustrating if you are not organized and does take time. Package your supplementary materials in any way as long as they are safe. I would say keep it as simple as possible and focus on the content. I sent my supplementary materials in manila envelopes with pre-printed addresses on the front of the envelope.

In this way, you physically and mentally create a bridge between your written application and your supplementary materials.

Now how do you create the final bridge between written application between written application, supplementary materials, and interview? This is done primarily by a thorough read your written material — your application (including your essays and "open" prompt responses) and your supplementary materials — before your interview. Read "The Interview" for more ideas on preparing for the interview. But here the focus is on your presentation during the interview — not actually what you are going to say, which is the focus of "The Interview".

Recognize how you presented yourself throughout your application. Whichever niche and whatever theme you have presented, make sure to be organized, polished, and passionate. These three traits are apparent in any successful college application. Likewise, these three traits should be apparent in your interview.

Provide your interviewer with a physical copy of your resume and your supplementary materials. Beforehand prepare for every interview by creating **interview packets** that can be standardized. These can be created after you create your **application-supplement packets** that we described above. Do not confuse yourself by doing both at the same time. Supplements should be sent soon after the electronic submission of your application. **Interview packets** can be created during winter break or in early January after all written information has been sent to universities.

Providing interviewers with **interview packets** serves four practical purposes. First, it allows interviews to be presented with information that you might talk about during the interview and also to remember you by a physical reminder after the interview. Third, the packet shows that you are organized and truly care about X University.

This approach allows you to focus on each aspect of the process one at a time and complete each thoroughly. It also gives you ample time to reflect on the process while you do it and to think about aspects like presentation that you might not have otherwise have had the time to.

Essays
- Personal Writing
- Showing passion

Supplements
- Showing passion through activity
- Verifying activities

Interview
- Showing passion through articulation

THE ELECTRONIC PRESENTATION

In today's digital world, a digital presence is both necessary and most probably reviewed in the application process. It is very easy to determine someone's reputation by a simple Google search of their name and perhaps school. This chapter is devoted to understanding how to regulate your digital presence and USE it to your advantage.

There are horror stories about students who have drunk pictures all over Facebook that admissions counselors find and then they are revoked admission or not offered it in the first place. I am sure this happens, and so it is necessary to regulate what goes on the Internet, and more importantly, WHAT YOU DO. Make sure that you are always in your sensible mind—I know I may sound like your mother here, but think about it yourself, it makes sense.

Let's get beyond defaming oneself on the Internet. Often, if you know you did something bad, it will be one of the first Google results and you should clean it up, as to say. There is nothing special about that.

The Internet can also be an OPPORTUNITY, instead of a risk. That is how winners, optimists, and successful college applicants think. Create a Facebook account that is clean and that is representative of who you are and what you do. Create a Twitter account. If you have created a nonprofit or a for-profit business, have Facebook and Twitter pages for these. If you have a band create a MySpace music profile for it and upload your songs.

If you have a blog then make sure it representative of who you are and what you do. If you do not, create one if you have the time! Outline your college admissions process, if anything, or your philosophies on life. Being technologically active and showing that you have a vibrant, open mind are often key qualities to a successful applicant.

The important thing is that you brand yourself: create a persona that is genuinely that "best" you and what you do. Be professional but also be honest and genuine. Like much of the process, this part is a little paradoxical, especially if you look at the few lines above. But achieving that balance is an art and the only way to do so is if you try.

PART 5: SHOWING PERSONALITY AND SHARING YOUR STORY

AN INTRODUCTION TO THE ESSAY

The essay is arguably the *most important* part of your application. By writing great college admissions essays ,you can increase your chances of acceptance and learn about yourself, writing, and emotions. Also the essay allows you to fit yourself in a certain way — by doing activities we develop passions and who we are. Writing specifically about who we are — with a unified **theme** — is critical to the process. Essay writing is a key aspect of *The Applicant* and deservedly so.

Develop passion for anything, just something at least

Show that passion through writing, interview, and activities

Be genuine and emotional so that others can see your passion as if it were their own

Ideally, the earlier writers (regardless of age — I consider 5th graders "writers") get exposed to the idea and importance of writing, the better. Over the years, each of us develops our own *art* of writing, termed our style. This style helps to communicate who we are and how we think. Realizing aspects of this style can help a writer manipulate and enunciate themselves, which tends to be critical in college especially.

The key of the college admissions essay is **personal writing:** exposition that focuses on your emotions, your beliefs, and your thought processes.

In high school and even in middle school, we are taught to write about a book or some topic that is removed from us, and analyze that topic. This approach to writing is NOT what colleges are looking for. They are looking to get to know YOU better, and the best way to do that is to write about yourself.

To practice **personal writing,** I have highlighted what I request my students to do and what I request you to do:

1. Read for 30 minutes once a week at least and right after **free write** for 10 minutes.
    a. What to read?
        i. I recommend reading New York Times or LA Times, or if you have a book that you would like to read (nonfiction or fiction) you can read that too.
    b. What to write? A **free write** is meant to be personal and creative, but often we have trouble when we start because we are not used to being so open-minded.

This is meant to help you when you first start.

    i. Think of your favorite childhood memory and write for ten minutes about it. Do not take time to plan out your work. Just write.

    ii. Write about your emotions or your beliefs. It is hard at first, but gets easier with time. Once every two weeks, look back and review what you wrote.

    iii. Write poems. Poems are one of the most direct paths into emotions.

    iv. Write a summary of what you just read.

    v. Every two weeks, critically analyze the books you enjoy reading and your writings. Analyze the writing styles of these authors. Often times, we imitate the style of writers we like and that forms the base for our own writing style.

2. Subscribe to a "Word a Day" email list and read that word to build your vocabularystudent

Another tactic that you can use is to first imagine your **ideal admissions officer**. Who would you want to read your essays and judge your "fit", if you could decide who this is? Now think about your choice. For me, it was a young man or woman who had just finished the admissions process and who understood all of the challenges I faced. He was optimistic and saw that I have visions and dreams. This reflected my own qualities: my youthfulness, energy, vision, and optimism. In the same way, reflect on who yours would be. This is a good way to begin thinking about who you are and a way to focus generalities into specifics. Just like in your activities and on your resume, **specificity** is key in your essays as it gives you immediate legitimacy and shows that you sincerely *thought* about your examples before using them. This in turn shows that you spent time on your applications and that you *care*.

I did this exercise with peers in high school and was introduced to the method by one of my favorite teachers of all time, Dr. Schultheis of Oak Park High School.

THE COLLEGE ADMISSIONS ESSAY

The successful college applicant is able to turn several sheets of paper — the Common Application or a similar document — into a living, breathing person. This is done by *the essay*. By practicing **personal writing** the applicant is able to write lively and significant essays efficiently and effectively. In high school and even in middle school we are taught to write about a book or some academic subject, which is different than what college admissions essays are asking for. In the admissions process, admissions officers are looking to get to know the applicant, the person, rather than their opinions or their activities even. Often times we write about our activities to impress admissions officers — they can see right through that. We write about our activities to show who we are indirectly. While this method is good, the successful essays augment this indirect approach with a direct approach — **personal writing**. Through this approach, we learn to show instead of tell. Instead of telling that you "like to play tennis" show it through your writing, "night or day, rain or shine, I play tennis."

The Successful College Admissions

Essay Components

Specificity

- Allows readers to grasp what you are saying
- Legitimacy in your claims
- *Shown through activities*

Honesty

- Shows you are a person rather than a paper
- *Shown through personal writing*

Passion

- *Shown through imagery*

Linkage

- Connecting activities and emotions to who you are
- Creating a multi-facted individual by showing different aspects

THE SHORT RESPONSE

There are also a number of short response questions on the Common Application and especially on the supplements for many schools. These short responses questions are limited by word count or schools specifically state "in about one paragraph" or something similar. They are critical and the right approach is important in sending a cohesive message to admissions officers.

The logic is the same: admissions officers want to know more about you, so write about yourself. For the short response, we have even fewer words to describe ourselves or a particular aspect of ourselves, so we must be even more direct. By using **I-statements**, such as "I stay late at the basketball court, the first to come to practice and the last to leave, practicing free throws", you can show your passion for something specific and be direct. These statements are key for the short response.

Sometimes prompts are so short they ask for just a few words. For example, Stanford University has had the question: "What five words best describe you?" for many years. The character count on this question, and similar questions, allow for more than just five words to be written down, so it becomes the writers choice whether to describe his/her choices or simply write five words. I don't think it makes much of a difference, as long as the five words truly describe you and are well thought-out, like "pensive".

The key to these essays is to be as direct and true to yourself as you can be. In addition to **I-statements** try to keep thoughts clean and simple. With a character count of 300, for example, you can only write a few sentences.

For the very short responses, try to convey one or two characteristics about yourself, if you are asked an open-ended question. In the slightly longer short responses, feel free to convey different aspects of yourself. In any case, it is important to maintain a theme throughout the application and the short responses, while being multi-faceted and not pointed.

THE PROMPT

There are a number of ways to approach the introduction, but all have the same end goal: focus the reader in on a specific topic and introduce yourself.

The essay is a *conversation* with admissions officers recorded in ink. It is a permanent record, and that is why colleges emphasize it in applications. They want to have a meaningful conversation with you, so they want you to write many essays.

Just like a conversation, the introduction is important in establishing a general mood.

Before starting to even write, there are some pre-writing protocols that I follow that you may find useful:

1. Review your previous writings: Recall that I suggested you write daily for 10 minutes uninterrupted every day. Review these entries.
   a. Try to find a common theme in your entries. Look for positives, avoid the theme: I am always so stressed. Are you optimistic? Are you hopeful for humanity or your family? Look for bigger themes.
   b. Identify your style. Do you write in longer, emphatic statements or shorter, succinct lines? Do you write in a scientific style with many –isms or do you write directly with non-inverted clauses? Try to identify this style, but if you cannot, do not worry. You

will find it by writing your college essays —
another benefit of this *opportunity*.

2. Take 5 minutes to sit and think. No music, no
Facebook, no distractions. Focus on what you are
about to do. You are about to have a conversation
with some people who are trying to see if you fit
into their school. Be yourself, but be your best self.
Sit and close your eyes. Think about yourself. This
may sound absurd, but it really cleared my mind
and it may clear yours too. I did some of my best
writing after doing this meditation and self-
examination.

The prompt can promote a certain type of essay, which I
have categorized into the **Essay Honeycomb** below.

1. "Creative prompts" are totally based on you and
focus on your emotions, who you are, and
sometimes even how you interpret a prompt. This
kind of essay is a pure **personal response**, based on
you.

2. "Structured prompts" focus on mixing in details
about the university you are applying to or details
about another subject, such as a person, into who
you are. These prompts usually require some in-
depth research and thinking into yourself.

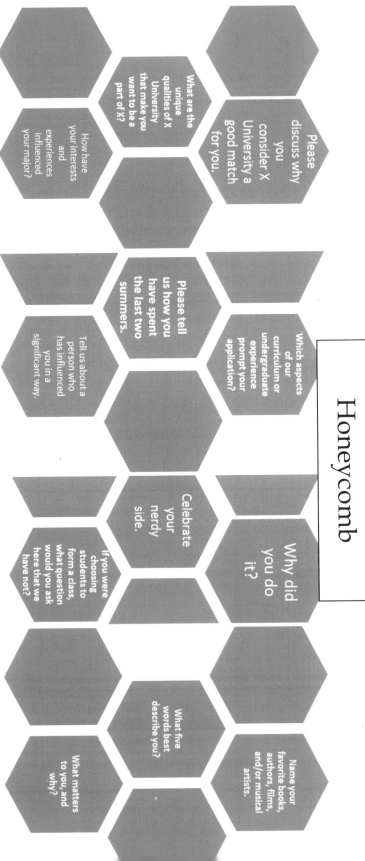

The Essay Honeycomb

Structured

What are the unique qualities of X University that make you want to be a part of X?

How have your interests and experiences influenced your major?

Please discuss why you consider X University a good match for you.

Please tell us how you have spent the last two summers.

Tell us about a person who has influenced you in a significant way.

Which aspects of our curriculum or undergraduate experience prompt your application?

Celebrate your nerdy side.

If you were choosing students to form a class, what question would you ask here that we have not?

Why did you do it?

What five words best describe you?

What matters to you, and why?

Name your favorite books, authors, films, and/or musical artists.

Creative

Real essay examples from Stanford, Tufts, Yale, and Emory.

Generally, prompts can be grouped:

1. The Research Prompt
    a. These prompts require you are also called the purely **structured prompt**. Often, these can help you decide if you like the atmosphere, social, and academic aspects of a university. They require heavy online research, perhaps emails to some **benchmark faculty members**, and review of materials that universities send home. They are some of the most pre-writing intensive prompts but also some of the most important to universities — which explains their nearly ubiquitous nature.
        i. Instead of just citing facts from the website try really *showing* your interest instead of telling:
            1. Contact students from your high school and ask them what their favorite experience was, and talk to them about the student life and similar facets.
            2. Contact professors who have done research you are interested. In your essay, discusses the *length* you have been in contact, the specific name, and why you are interested.

3. Contact some specific clubs, talk about your interest in them and maybe how your activities in the past show your interest. For example, having done dance for several years, you can show that you would become a part of X dance troupe.

4. Write about very specific details instead of broad generalizations. Avoid talking about the "strong science programs" or "interdisciplinary work". Instead, talk about Stanford's IHUM Program and Making of the Modern World, a specific course that interests you because it combines history with modernity through the lens of primary texts.

2. The Reflection Prompt

a. These prompts are a mix between the **structured prompt** and the **creative prompt**. They make you reflect on who you are and what you have done. Many of my high school friends complained about this prompt because they had nothing they thought was *significant* to write about. Their approach is wrong — there is always something or someone who has significantly shaped who you are, regardless if you have won national championships or enjoy spending time with your father. If you are a senior reading this and writing your essays right now, there is little to do but make sure your *attitude* is positive. There were COUNTLESS fellow classmates who undermined themselves by conveying an under confident aspect in their essays. This aspect bled into their style, their essays, and eventually their interviews. These essays are proof of the method I have outlined in a previous chapter about resume-building and activity-building.

    i.   You first need to brainstorm who and what has influenced who you are. Also, you need to think about who you are, of course.

    ii.   Once you have identified someone or something, think about *how* they have influenced you. It could be that your father made sure to come to every one of your football games, and showed you the value of family. It could be anything, but it has to be genuine and honest.

    iii.   Combine some facts/events, such as the ones you found in part (ii) about *how* you have been influenced, with who you are. The reflection prompt is a mixture of facts/events and who you are .

3. The Creativity Prompt

    a. These prompts make you *think*. They are the **creative prompt.** For some of these prompts, I took two days just to develop a kernel idea. I mulled over how to approach the prompt and how to answer it to develop some aspect of myself.

        i. You have to focus on who you are, not even what you have done to show that. Who are you? Try to free write to discover yourself. These are the easiest prompts because they are so open-ended, and the hardest because they require you to look inside of yourself.

    b. This is the one exception where I think one sort of distraction should be allowed, namely, music. I consider myself musical, and I write these kinds of essays better with music because it allows me to tap into my creativity. If you are similarly-oriented, you can try to listening to music and writing these kinds of prompts.

We will now look at a very common prompt, the Why Us essay prompt, to give you a more tangible idea of what we are talking about. The Why Us essay prompt falls under the Research prompt, and requires understanding of the university and why you think you fit in. It is a critical essay that every school tries to ask in some way or another.

Case Study: The Why Us Essay

Why do you want to come to X University?

Let us go back to Student A and B:

Student A: Dude, I have two days to write all my essays! Why did I leave it to the last minute. I am going to "lockdown" myself and just write for 10 hours today. My parents will be relieved and I will get this done. Let me update my Facebook status first: Essay time! I am going to be off of Facebook for the rest of the week. After doing this, Student A turns of his/her phone and opens the Common Application and the Supplement. After quickly filling in his name and basic information he moves to his first supplement:

Student B: Ok, I have two and a half months to do write out who I am. I filled out the information on the Common Application two days ago, so now I can fully focus on the essays and the prompts. The prompt is:

Why do you want to come to X University?

Student A: Hmm, this should be easy. Come on, hurry up! Ok I got it. I want to go to X University because the weather is so nice and obviously the people are nice. I also want to go here because I have heard that it has a wonderful Economics department and I am interested in Economics. I think these reasons are sufficient. Ok, let me fluff my essay up now. It will be fine. My interview will be worth *more*

I will be *honest* with you now: I know countless students who did this. They whizzed by their essays and spent a concentrated amount of time before essays were due writing furiously. Some had good results, but most did not because they really did not put their *heart* into the conversation. They did not have a deep conversation; they only scratched the surface of who they are. This situation is unfortunate, because some very smart, unique individuals get caught in this bubble and lower their own chances of admission.

Time is what causes some students to get caught in this **time bubble**, as I will call it. For a few intensive days, students work in this bubble but they cannot see outside of it. They superficially answer the essay prompts, complete the applications, but they do not put their *heart* into the process. After reading "The Philosophy/The Perspective Method", I hope you understand what this heart is and why it is important to put *yourself* into the process, to embrace it.

Student B: Ok. So why did X University ask this question out of all possible questions? They want to know why I applied here as opposed to other schools. What do I think makes them unique? This can help them identify the perception of their school in the general public. But they also know I have chosen to apply to their school because I can see myself *living, growing, and contributing* in a healthy way. Why can I see myself there? They want to know what kind of profile student their school attracts and what I can offer. Why do I fit in?

This critical approach to the very simple, succinct, and common question will yield insightful answers and an unusual essay. By starting the process in a thoughtful and provoking way, the essay *itself* becomes insightful.

Now that the philosophy of the approach has been laid out, what about the practical aspects? How can I answer this question?

For me, this question asks me to research X University. The key here is **specificity.** The level of detail that you can research an institution and get to know it largely determines how others perceive your *drive* and *want* to attend X University. In addition, this research process can help you determine if you want to spend this much time applying and if it truly is a fit for you and not just another school you have decided to apply to. This is how I approach the research process:

1. Visit the school's website. Read their mission statement and about their history. Who were significant individuals who grew from their institution?
   a. Researching the Academics
      i. Read the "about" pages from every department you are *vaguely interested in.* These "about" pages can give you an idea about the leaning of the department. For example, MIT's Economics Department may be considered more math-oriented than Columbia's.
      ii. Read the Academic Philosophy of the school, if it has such a page. Sometimes this is integrated into the history of the

school or another informational page located on the general website.

iii. Look for peculiarities within each school in regards to academics. These nuances can help you identify the personality of the school—the subject you will be conversing about with the admissions officers through your essay. For example, Stanford has an Honor Code that trusts students not to cheat on exams to the extent that professors leave the testing area when the exam begins. This shows the amount of trust Stanford has in its students and the responsibility it is willing to give them. This attitude, from my perspective, also carries on to other parts of the school. In such a way, search for these peculiarities. They become points of interests in the interview as well—giving the interviewer an idea of the amount of time you spent research and the *commitment* you have to the school.

iv. Finally, try and find what I call **benchmark faculty members**.

These are the faculty members who are known by most of the students at X University, for their eccentricity, teaching ability, or some other unusual aspect. I would research these individuals, perhaps look at some of their papers or writings, and see if any of them particularly strikes a note with me.

b. Researching Extracurricular Activities on Campus

    i. Look for a directory of student clubs on campus. Most universities have this directory or some kind of search menu. Read through the various organizations and see if any *truly* excite you. If they do, make sure to note them and perhaps mention them in your essays. **Specificity** is key here. Really look into the clubs, and if you truly like one, perhaps email the junior or senior in charge of the club asking them about it. This search and your efforts will not go to waste. Your passion will be evident in some way — whether it is in the interview or essays.

      ii. Try and find any school-sponsored events that occur yearly or for a specific class. These many times determine "school spirit" and are hallmarks of the X University College Experience.

During this process, collect your ideas onto paper or in an electronic document. Make notes, hyperlink specific pages that interest you, and then simulate.

Simulate yourself at the university, as a college freshman. Simulate yourself living with dorm mates, eating meals together, going to class, and repeating the exercise. Write these notes down in another electronic document. First, they will be interesting to look at when you go to college. Second, they are the real substance of a great college essay on why you want to attend X University.

The Why Us essay is important because that is ultimately what colleges want to know, through you application. In a poll from College Confidential of 6,286 students, "Good vibes" came in at 36%. "Good vibes" means good fit—which is part of the Why Us. Students recognize the importance of feeling at home, and so do admissions officers.

ew Poll Results: What is the most impt factor in selecting a college?

estige, overall academic ranking or reputation.

:ademic strength in my intended major.

:ography: close enough to home.

:ography: far away enough from home.

mate.

iition, potential scholarships and cost of living.

gacy status/family history at the school.

lfriend/boyfriend, other friends there.

hletics.

od vibes...felt at home.

n College Confidential

Multiple Choice Poll. Voters: **6286.** You may not vote on this

Approach each prompt with similar notions. I chose this particular prompt because it is very common and is one that requires some of the most pre-writing preparation. Other prompts will require pre-writing and a lot of rewriting. Realize every essay prompt is a critical part of the conversation in which admissions officers learn about how you *interpret* a question. There is no right or wrong answer, just a not-so-passionate and passionate response.

THE INTRODUCTION

Now are you are ready to write. If you have identified the way in which you think and your style there are two options that you have to decide between:

1. Just start writing. For you, writing is an organic process that comes and you have an analytical mind and a specific style (perhaps long-winded and detail-oriented). Take points from your simulation document and incorporate them. Remember, **specificity** is key to a persuasive essay.
2. Formulate an outline, incorporating points you developed from your simulation and from your points on the school.

Both methods are effective—it just depends on what kind of writer you are. Both can create equally effective essays.

There are a few things to keep in mind when writing. Please look up again at the chapter "The College Admissions Essay" for the four key components before writing:

1. A **Theme**: People like stories (yes, admissions officers are people too). Telling someone a story (remember the essay is a conversation) will draw them in and can also tell them about who you are and how you think. One of the most clichéd recommendations is to have a theme in your essays, and I reiterate that. It is almost necessary.

But I will extend that thematic aspect to your *entire* application. I will expand on this later.

2. Be Yourself. Just be natural and convey who you really are. Do not try to fit into that typical "nerd" or "jock" role. If you have followed the guidelines of working in high school and the tips in regarding extracurricular activities and grades, you will be fine. If you have taken these steps, you will not be the "I am good at many things, but not great at any" stereotype. Believe me, *a majority* of students fall in this unfortunate category. They really have not honed their skills.

3. Be conscious of your style, but not too conscious. Let the words flow to you. Do not package yourself by superficially adding words here and there to make yourself sound "smarter". But if you have a loquacious style, let it go. Make sure in this case to read over your work though. It really does not help to package yourself stylistically and admissions officers can read right through it.

4. Get yourself in the writing mood. This could be listening to music before and during the writing process, doing a little mediation, exercising, reading, or even sleeping. Everyone has their own preparation. Let me give you the example of myself.

    a. I always take a 30 minute power nap before working from 4:30 PM to 5:00 PM. Sometimes my best writing occurred right after waking up. I never thought that this could be, but after rereading my essays I wrote after just waking up I was surprised.

Another tactic I used was going on a 30 minute walk outside while listening to music before writing. This cleared my mind and allowed me to write clearly.

This writing process is beautiful because it is a combination of creativity and concrete theory. It is a combination of grammar and style. This conversation you have with admissions officers should communicate *you*. On my last of numerous read-throughs of my essays, I would see the big picture. Does the essay communicate *me?* When I was satisfied that it did, I submitted happily and stress-free.

THE HEART OF THE ESSAY

I cannot advise you on the particulars of writing your essay. The content of your essays should reflect you—that is about as specific as I can get. Make sure that you answer the prompt with concrete examples and with your personality—the latter which should be evident with your writing style and your thinking process.

There are a few key aspects that the successful essay should have, developed in the heart of the essay:

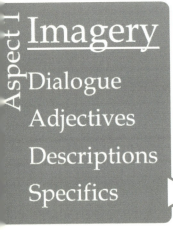

Aspect 1 — **Imagery**: Dialogue, Adjectives, Descriptions, Specifics

Aspect 2 — **Honesty**: Personal Writing, True facts

Aspect 3 — **Active Voice**: Present Tense, Active verbs

When working on your essays, there are two ways of approach: complete one essay at a time via the **focused approach** or do bits of multiple essays and switch via the **dispersed approach**. I recommend the **dispersed approach** because it allows the writer to "refresh" mentality. Especially when it comes to the **dream school predicament**, students tend to focus on one essay for that particular dream school and spend days on that instead of completing essays to other schools. At the end of the day, the application process is a statistical chance and maybe that perfect essay in your eyes was not perfect to an admissions officer, another reason why the dream school predicament can lead to an overly **focused approach** and worse essays overall.

The **focused approach** is appropriate for writers who get distracted easily and must finish a task at once, however, students cannot spend all their time writing just a few of the essays. The **dispersed approach** is appropriate for any student, especially those that need mental "breaks" from the different types of prompts (see "Essay Honeycomb"). I highly recommend the **dispersed approach** especially if students are applying to many schools and if the schools they are applying to have low acceptance rates.

The heart of the essay consists of the body paragraphs. They should have the examples that you wish to convey and should draw from your experiences through your activities (perhaps you pinpoint one particular experience or a series). Usually, targeting specific incidents will increase the **specificity** of your essay, which is always a good thing. By choosing a specific incident, it implies that you have a plethora of experiences to choose from and you chose this one for its significance to you and its representative quality or extraordinary quality. Of course, you cannot have these specific experiences unless you have many — which is why it is important to have a central theme surrounded by many related activities, and why it is important to be a multi-faceted individual. Often, at the end of the writing process, **essay fatigue** can hit. This tiredness of the process can be fought by taking short strategic breaks, such as taking a shower or going for a run, and by also reminding yourself that after the deadline, around the beginning of January, the process is out of your hands. Taking full control of what you can change will give you the strength to continue writing.

Besides specific experiences, you may also choose to write on a specific moment in a competition. These moment-based essays usually focus on the dedication it took to reach that point and the passion you have that drove you to reach that high point. Many times, these moment-based essays can revolve around your **"big thing"**.

THE EDITING PROCESS

The editing process is as important as writing in the essay writing experience. The key to the editing process is *knowing* yourself and knowing when you have accurately portrayed who you think you are in your essays. When you feel that you have accurately conveyed yourself, you are done with the process. I know the problem with this approach, as I am a "perfectionist" as some of you are too: editing has the potential to never end. You never feel that the essay is *ready*. But trust me, if you allow enough time to brainstorm, write, and review your essays, you will be *ready*. I reviewed some of my essays over twenty times, but at some point I felt I was done and had conveyed my ideas and myself completely.

There are a few aspects of the editing process:

1. Content
    a. Read through your rough drafts identifying what you think the theme of the essay and your application is as if you were the admission officer. Are you conveying what you are thinking? I think everyone needs work here — numerous times I found that when I had others read my essays, they did not get the message I was thinking. This is a *one-sided conversation*.
    b. This first editing tip ties hand-in-hand with idea of having peer revision and other editors. It is EXTREMELY important to have others read your essays. Ask them,

what is the theme of my application? What does this paragraph convey or what does this essay say to you? These are important, broad questions that must be answered similarly by many readers in order to ensure that you will probably convey the same ideas to the admissions officers.

2. Grammar

   a. Next, and equally important, is analysis of your grammar. Grammar is like the flow of the conversation — without proper grammar the conversation is halted and stilted. Even if the content of the conversation is brilliant, the stilted aspect will hinder your entire application and may give false impressions to admissions officers.

   b. There are a few ways to have your grammar revised:

      i. Have others read for your essays and prompt them to particularly look for grammar mistakes. You can term these individuals **grammar readers**. They skip over content usually. It is usually better to differentiate the readers and not let them overlap in one sitting.

      ii. If you are younger (e.g. 9th, 10th, or 11th grade) then you start improving your own grammatical skills, which will be *very* useful for the writing part of the SAT and for your future writing career. There are grammar books you can read in local libraries or bookstores. Also, the Internet is a great source for understanding grammar. As always, mix these readings into your daily readings and make sure you continue to write 10 minutes uninterrupted every day. This slew of strategies will not only improve your writing and reading abilities but also your thinking process.

3. Style
   a. Now that you have reviewed the most important aspects of your essays, look at your style. As we discussed, *style* is the way you hold the conversation and helps reveal who you really are. Do you speak loquaciously (long sentences, many nouns and adjectives) or concisely? Both styles are perfectly acceptable as long as you communicate fully what you want to be communicating.
      i. There are a few ways to analyze your style:
         1. Read your essays specifically looking at *how* you write your essays. For me, this was done by almost skimming my essays, looking at the repeating structures within sentences and throughout the essay.

2. If you find a sentence, a phrase, or a word that is peculiar and sticks out compared to the rest of your essay, try to find why it is unusual. This method can also help you indirectly discover your style.

After doing looking at these three components of your essays, you will have read your essays dozens and dozens of times over and over. You might even have partially memorized your essays at this point.

Another key of the review process: TAKE BREAKS. Do something else from time to time, make sure that you give yourself time to get out of the "editing" mindset and then return in slightly different settings, at a slightly different time, with a slightly different temperament. This activity can be anything: exercising, painting, talking, or even sleeping. Just remember to change the tone and atmosphere before returning to review. Sometimes, I felt that I hit a **reviewing block** because I did not take a break. You will now when one of these blocks is coming on when you start to say the same things to yourself about the same line, even if you have changed that line. This phenomenon means that you are starting to edit with a similar mindset. At this point you should take a break. Reviewing is so necessary and is one of the main reasons I suggest that you start writing your essays earlier: more time to review.

Reviewing your essays like this will give you so much more depth and perspective. It is an art. This is also a fault of doing your essays all at once: the review process is also squished. Some writers say that the review process is even more important that the actual writing. While you may or may not agree with this, know at least that is an *entirely* separate process that requires time, energy, and **focus**. You should be so familiar with your essays that you can almost expect what is coming next.

I reviewed my essays at least five times each before submission. I just want to give you reference. Obviously, you do not have to review your essays thirty times, but you should also review your essays more than once.

SAMPLE ESSAYS

Below I have included some sample essays that are exemplary in showing a specific aspect that has been discussed above. First, read the essay and then the comments following.

Energy

"Yes, that in the distance is the Sydney Harbor Bridge" my cousin tells me as we stroll in the middle of the city on a crisp Thursday morning.

The locals scramble to work and giant Ferris of steel await departure. But something catches my attention: an unusually low growl, the sound of a didgeridoo. I follow the music and find an aboriginal man playing. Instantly I want to learn as I become encapsulated in the sound and feel of Australian culture firsthand.

Before coming back to America to attend the new school year--the 10th grade--I luckily find a didgeridoo to purchase. It joins my collection of instruments; among the most unusual are tabla, dhol, dholki, and sitar.

The didgeridoo is especially important to me, however. I enjoy the challenge of learning from YouTube videos, from my own ear, and from the oral tradition of playing passed down each generation. In a way, my passion for curiosity and adventure is manifested in this instrument. I must explore how to play, experiment how to hold the instrument. The music itself allows me to experience another culture.

As I sit down to blow on the didgeridoo, I close my eyes and play whatever whim comes to my mind. I began to hear musical patterns in my head, and I imitate them in reality. As I begin to hear my sound, I communicate my emotions to the world. I give a part of myself to the car whizzing by outside, to the stove, and to my mom who is cooking lunch. After some time, I turn to the dhol, a two-sided drum from rural Punjab that is handed down from elders of each generation. Loose turns of my wrist result in resonating "booms" as I coordinate the two drum heads and the two sticks: one a thin flattened bamboo-like piece and the other a thick J-shaped wooden rod. Energy passes through me, my hands become nimble and my heart starts to beat faster.

Music is always around me: whether I am hearing the construction tractors roll along in Los Angeles or the hummingbird sip from a flower. This universality makes me comfortable to tap out a beat on the table with my fingers or hum a tune during dinner. Many times I pick up rhythms by my ear, without training. Other times I use my experience to dissect a piece: "Mom, I can hear the bass, drums, guitar, and trumpet playing in unison here."

In any case, music, whether it be prepared or natural, gives me inner peace because I can connect with other human beings. I can express myself by snapping my fingers or giving sharp rhythmic taps on the tabla. Playing these foreign instruments allows me to tap into a dynamic energy and relate to other people, other cultures, and gain a different perspective on the world and on music. I cherish the journey of struggling to learn on my own, I revel in being lost and finding my way. In many ways, music is who I am.

Analysis: This is a good essay, exceptional in showing passion and using imagery to convey that message. Here is an example of how to paint a picture: "The locals scramble to work and giant Ferris of steel await departure." You can literally imagine the scene, and you even imagine yourself there. By setting the scene early, the writer is able to capture the reader's attention *and* show how important that initial contact with the didgeridoo was. Through that imagery, he is able to passion for music instead of saying "I really enjoy music". He links his passion for music to some character traits as well: spontaneity and initiative, taking the chance to see who is playing the didgeridoo and learning how to play from YouTube. His honest is proven through his consistent writing style and imagery, his passion for music effuses throughout this essay through personal writing and the use of "I". Finally, the writer is specific about what he is talking about and the reader can grasp that through the essay.

In My Room

It started with a 5th grade teacher and has grown into a lifestyle. I look around me: PDF papers are spread out on my desk and on the carpet floor, red ink and highlighter marks scrawled hastily on them. Popular Science and

Wired magazines sit on top of my dresser and on my printer. My computer has small sticky notes with many equations. My whiteboard has the one critical equation. Research has become a part of me.

But today's expression grew out a lifetime of curiosity and discovery. As a toddler, my parents tell me that I used to try all foods--even snails from the ground. As a seven year-old I mixed soap, eucalyptus leaves, Windex, and even a gumball together to create an air freshener that I marketed to one customer--Wolfgang, my seventy year-old neighbor. My curiosity was next nourished by Dr. Dunn, a motherly science teacher who forced us to do a science project in 5th grade. One day when I was researching possible projects in middle school, I realized that I was feeling something inside of me: happiness.

I have followed that feeling and spark up to today. In 10th grade my Spanish teacher inspired me to look beyond class and eventually into linguistics. I fell in love with linguistics and decided to enter a linguistics paper into the science fair. No one from Ventura County had won 1st place in any division at the California State Science Fair in 8 years. Many of my teachers did not even know how science fairs worked. But I was determined to turn my interest into a science project, even if it meant that I had to find my own way. After months of emailing scores of professors across the country who could mentor me, I found a UCLA professor, whom I have been researching with for 2 years in the field of computational linguistics. With his help, I wrote a research paper that let me speak with ex-governors and allowed me to present my findings at the London International Youth Science Forum and across California. But more importantly, I have been able to turn that brief moment of happiness that I had in 5th grade into my continuing love of research.

As I stand now looking at my whiteboard, with an equation no one in the world has seen before--my equation--that feeling bubbles up again. This equation has taken me two years of computational linguistics research to derive, but I believe it is an expression 17 years in the making. Looking around me, I see that my science project is just another manifestation of my love of science, a love I have been pursuing all my life. Gyroscopes, NASA-authorized space pens, a tube with my first isolated wheat germ DNA, and countless books were all hints to me. They are hidden in the room I stand in now, but they have lead me to the treasure: my equation on the whiteboard.

Then I think again: this equation is yet another hint about my future, it is not the treasure. The treasure is not some novel equation, award, or science paper. The treasure is the opportunity to pursue my love of research. This room helped me find what the treasure is, the next room, my dorm room, will help me live it as I pursue my love of research at the university level.

Analysis: The imagery in this essay is strong, but the linkage is the biggest strength of this essay. From a simple equation, the writer here is able to turn his room into a looking glass for his entire life, into what he does and who he is, focusing on the second particularly. He connects past with present resoundingly, especially at the end "This room helped me find what the treasure is, the next room, my dorm room..." to bring continuity to his story. Another reason why this is a strong essay is because the author understands that winning a competition is not for the sake of writing something more on the resume but is a natural extension of his passion for research. It is a specific essay, focusing on his equation and his dorm room, so the reader can wrap his/her head around the material. Finally, the essay bring forth honesty through its continuity and direct approach to telling the motive behind entering competitions: as an extension of who the writer is.

Roommate Essay

Ying and yang. In many ways I am a paradox, but I think that's what makes me interesting. Spontaneous I follow my whim, paint, draw, roam the city and get lost. I have become lost in London, Boston, and Melbourne walking the streets during solo travels. But it was adventure. But then I am disciplined, sitting down to study everyday at 5:00 PM, systematically taking off my watch, closing Facebook and my cell phone. On one hand I follow this routine, and then on the other I push my limits--zip-lining in the forest, tasting escargot, and even trying kangaroo meat. Food, yes, that brings me to another point. I like my fettuccini alfredo and cheeseburgers. I can live with these for years. But I love trying new foods: anything slimy, prickly, sour, or tangy can enter my mouth.

Because of my openness I attract others and others attract me; I love making friends. Life is to be lived all the way up, isn't it? Along my journey so far I have met Douglases from Jamaica, Maias from Israel, Jacks from New Zealand, Natalias from Peru and many more. Each one makes me a little fuller, adding a little more ying and a drop of yang.

Maybe the one constant is that I squeeze every drop of meaning and life out of every moment. Whether the task is eating, studying, having fun, or volunteering, I throw myself into it with no inhibitions. Life is a test which we can never fail. That's why I want to push myself in everything I do. That's why I want to go skydiving. This is the most important part of me: passion. If I am accepted to Stanford University, I will soak in the experience and envelope myself in the faculty, my peers, and the atmosphere.

Dear roommate, what are your interests? What do you do for fun? What do you want to study?

I look forward to diving into college with you.

Analysis: The author draws clear parallels between what he likes to eat and who he is. In this way, linkage is strong. This essay's strength is in its specificity and imagery: focusing on "kangaroo meat" and "fettuccini alfredo" the author is able to paint a realistic, honest, and imaginable picture of what he likes to eat. The subject itself is unique but very thought-provoking: what we eat does show who we are, but we often take that fact for granted. In this way, the author has shown that he has put thought before writing the essay, showing the importance of pre-writing. The author again shows honesty through his direct approach, "This is the most important part of me:

passion." By being straightforward and honest, he is able to paint a picture of an amiable, passionate roommate that can listen and wants to enjoy his experience at Stanford University.

THE INTERVIEW

By this stage, you have taken the SAT or ACT, developed your theme, your niche, written, reviewed, and submitted your essays and your application. Take a deep breath. You have really done a lot of work. Remember that every single positive step you take will add up over time and show your passion. It will come through. If you have done these steps, you have devoted most of your time in high school to positive, constructive tasks that concretely demonstrate who you are and what you want to be seen as. Now it is the time for the interview.

Some students overly concern themselves with the interview. If there is one key aspect of the interview it is to:

BE YOURSELF.

You are unique, and you have developed a theme that demonstrates a particular aspect that you wish to convey. First, I will repeat, be yourself. You have interacted with other people for 17, 18, or 19 years and you know who you are: maybe you are detail-oriented, very particular about your breakfast, or a really fun person to be around. The interview is the "show off" period when you demonstrate to a representative of X University your passion, commitment, and understanding of the process.

To help you polish and clear yourself before the interview, I have a few tips:

a. One week or a few days before your interview, sit down at your desk. Remove all distractions (music, cell phone, Facebook etc.) and just sit and think for two minutes. Put the timer on your watch and close your eyes. Who are you? Try to answer this question in the two minutes.

b. Now write for five minutes in free form — write in whatever style you wish: paragraphs, phrases, poems, anything that you feel comfortable doing. Write down your major accomplishments and how they tell your story. Your story tells who you are, after all.

c. Once this process is over, read over your work. Who are you? Try to answer the question again with what you have written. Carefully consider the unconscious style choice you made to convey your ideas. What does this stylistic choice say about who you are?

d. Now look over your resume. Through which achievements, activities, and leadership positions does your theme most clearly shine through? Make sure to bring these up in your interview.

e. *Research the institution again.* Read the essays you wrote that required research. Now, re-read each institution's "about" page and recall any specific interesting facts about the university. Try to recognize the general attitude of the university as well. These facts *will* come in handy during the interview and help to show your interest in the university. They are done by about 40%

of students to some extent — but any way of differentiating yourself is good.

The idea behind these exercises is to tell the interviewer your story and your specific theme, whatever that may be. You developed your theme in your essays, which is why you should look over them before applying. Look over your **one-sentence approach** and be able to tell that in an engaging and personal manner. Finally, look at the "Why X University?" essays to find the reasons you truly found compelling about the University. Having followed the right approach to this question will be reinforced here, not simply saying, "The weather is nice in New York" or "The student body is diverse" is sufficient or believable.

Now you are ready for your interview. The day before your interview, look again over these aspects and the notes you made about what you want to convey. *The final key is confidence.* Go in to the interview knowing who you are and looking to convey your passion for each institution in the limited amount of time you have. At the same time, try to be as natural as possible. These interviewers are people too.

Now your interview is over. Most people give a sigh of relief, say that was not as bad as I expected, and never talk again to their interviewer or make contact. I would say that 90% of all students who have interviews do this.

The appropriate thing to do is send them a hand-written thank you letter—thanking them for their time and for a wonderful conversation. Make sure to also include specific points brought up in the conversation—remember **specificity** is still the key, even in the interview. I would say that at most 5% of students do this task.

I would shun away from an email, unless you do not have their physical address. If you do not have their address, send the email because it is better than not thanking them at all. Be sincere in your thanks; realize that they have other things they could be doing but are *volunteering* their time to interview you. Usually, interviewers also want the best for you. They are trying to determine your fit with their alma mater and are usually very friendly, open, and warm. Be open-minded during and after your interview and humble during the whole process.

PART 6: THE FINAL STRETCH

THE WAIT

After completing my interviews, the wait began. This is the seemingly long time between submitting all of applications and finishing interviews to getting the results. Indeed, I tried to keep myself busy with school and my extracurricular activities, but it is on every senior's mind until decision day.

First, just take a deep breath. I still remember that moment when I submitted the last of more than thirty applications. I knew inside that I had given everything I had and shown myself to the best of my abilities to the admissions officers. I knew luck would play a significant part in the admissions process and that is why I so heavily diversified. I felt satisfied. When you submit your last application and have your last interview, take a deep breath afterwards. Close your eyes. Imagine what you have just done. You have told your life story to many wise, older people how are going to determine if you should continue developing mentally, socially, and physically at their institution or at another. Recognize that you have given everything you have and relax.

I realize that this separation from the process becomes harder as the notification date approaches, and students again start talking about the process. At this point, you have had much time to focus on other activities. Still try to focus on your extracurricular activities because you have no control over the results now. Focus on what you can do: work on your school work and your extracurricular activities. Make sure that you stay unbiased toward your colleges at this point as emotions among your contemporaries start to get intermixed with results. This is the end of the race when true dedication is shown. Your fellow students will admire your leadership at this time and you should be proud of yourself if you continue as passionately as ever in your activities. Heroes are made when no one is watching. Work as hard as you have ever worked now. The results come soon, focus on something you can change.

Now let us be realistic. It will be on your mind if you let it. It was on mine sometimes, and this is perfectly normal. But do not paralyze yourself. DO NOT STOP YOUR EXTRACURRICULAR ACTIVITIES. I will repeat that: do not stop doing your extracurricular activities. Yes, it is the end of senior year and you have submitted your applications and technically no one will get to know if you continued writing for the school paper or not, but you will.

During this waiting process, you are the one who will be thinking about the decision. If you stop your activities, you will give yourself more time to idly sit around and think. Instead of brooding over the possibilities, do something constructive that you truly love! Think about it in the long term—you will have further developed your skills in a particular area and you will may have gained another **"big thing"** (for example, many prestigious science fair competitions continue into February and later).

Think about it. You are a senior. You have spent four years at your high school and you probably know most of the students at your school—or they know you. You are the top of your high school career, taking difficult AP/IB classes and managing a social life. Why waste it on idly sitting by not caring about classes? This is the time during which the biggest strides of success are shown. The culmination of your work in classes and your extracurricular activities occur now as you are the most experienced member of many of your clubs and organizations. You are the boss. But that does not mean that classes do not mean anything. Again, just like the freshman myth, the senioritis myth is FALSE.

THE MYTH OF SENIORITIS

Focus on your schoolwork. That horrible disease called seniorities does not really exist if you do not let it exist. There were some moments during my senior year during which I just wanted to give up. Moments—minutes of the day—that I remember now in disgust and laugh at. If there is one thing that I should have cherished more it is *time*. One can always make more money, more friends, have more lovers. But *time* leaves us forever.

REJECTED

This section is for students who have been rejected to one or more schools. This includes a majority of applicants and it included me. I will give you some ways to think about the schools that rejected you and the idea behind the rejection.

First: it does not mean that they *reject you*. It means that they do not feel that at this time, you are not a right fit for their university. Do not take the rejection personally. Try not to. It is natural, especially if you devote yourself to the process, to feel this way. There is a lot of luck in this process and perhaps just this time it did not go your way. Having applied to several schools will be a failsafe against having no college to attend.

In addition, if you have that can-do attitude, you will think ahead. Fine, they did not think I was the right fit right now. I will apply again for graduate school. I will be persistent. Persistence is a character trait all of us could use more of. Starting to develop it earlier would always be more beneficial. If you truly feel that the admissions officers have not seen you correctly and judged you the way that you want to be, file an appeal. What is the worst that could happen? They stand on their judgment. Just realize that for top schools appeals will usually not be granted. Realize that perhaps you really are not a fit at all schools and that the ones that accepted you really want you. They are extending an offer to you. They want you to be part of their legacy, of their name. They believe you will grow in so many ways at their university and will be a positive influence for other students. Look at the positives, and make sure not to shrug off the universities that rejected you. It is just that this time, during this read through by an admissions officer, he/she did not feel that you were a fit. No one decides your worth except you. Look forward, be confident, and start deciding between your acceptances which school you truly want to attend.

WAITLISTED

What should I do if I am waitlisted? I was waitlisted to a few schools and I used a few strategies to improve my chances. First you have to consider: do you still *really* want to attend X University that you are on the waitlist for? The chances of getting admitted off the waitlist, especially for top schools, are slim but still existent. If you really want to get off the waitlist you must show your passion for that particular school in an extraordinary and concrete way.

Let us now say that you have decided to stay on the waitlist. Many schools have a site in which you mark whether or not you want to be on the waitlist. This preference must usually be recorded soon after decisions are released. Be careful of this deadline.

So how do you continue to show your passion to the institution? Correspondence is necessary, through a brief but informative **update letter**. Notify the colleges of any achievement. This will let them know that you are still working hard and you are also truly passionate about what you do. It is also an excuse to send them a cover letter reiterating your desire to attend X University and your continued passion.

I must admit, this approach is taken by many students who are waitlisted, especially at top universities. If you do something extraordinary — such as hold a concert, film it, and then send it to the school which you sung about — you will receive attention. One of my friends did such an thing for Princeton, and although he was mentioned in the press release by Princeton disseminating final statistics for the Class of 2014, he was not admitted.

I would approach the waitlist almost as a rejection. This way, you will be surprised if you get in. But honestly do not count on the acceptance. Work passionately toward showing your love of an institution but make sure you choose carefully which schools to stay on the waitlist for because showing your passion can require a lot of time and effort that could be spent visiting the colleges you already got into or focusing on your classwork. Ultimately, the choice is yours. Remember that there is always further schooling and opportunities to pursue education at any institution outside of degree-granting programs.

Give yourself a pat on the back for getting onto the waitlist. You are part of an exclusive group of students that a university wants but does not have room for. They believe that other students have a better fit than you do for the institution but they also see the merits of your application. This is what is written on many waitlist letters and was told to me by a Harvard University admissions officer.

WHERE TO GO?

Now you have your acceptance letters. You have lived through the application process, embraced it, and survived the wait. You have truly embraced the process and completed it. First, be proud of yourself. You did it!

The results have come back. I remember the specific day that the results came back. They come as a flood — at the same time, for me near the end of a particular school day. Trying to remove yourself from the process becomes harder and harder as the date of notification comes closer. Now look at the results. They are usually one letter from each school. The first sentence or so will usually tell you the outcome. Do not be afraid to let out a shout of joy or a verbal sigh. Let it all come out now.

Now you have the choices. Now you can start being biased. Several people have spent hours reviewing your application, trying to learn who you are and what you stand for through your words and through accounts of the individuals who interviewed you. Rethink where you want to attend college now. Have any of your preferences changed in the few months, the waiting period, between sending your application and your results? If so, consider how these factors affect where you see yourself for the next four years. Again, consider the atmospheres of the institutions and perhaps visit a few of them.

This is where you have the chance to judge the schools and really find where you can see yourself. DO

NOT judge schools based on where your parents want you to go or on prestige or any other external factor.

One thing I looked at when judging schools was if students were smiling and seemed happy everywhere on campus. Did they interact with each other? Did they seem happy? Also I looked at the dorm atmosphere. It is very easy to get into the dorms, just ask a student to let you in. See what the *real* Blank University is like. This may be unorthodox but it was one of the most valuable things I did. See what life is like without all the preparation. Actually, it might sometimes be different than what you expect. For a few schools, the atmosphere was actually a little different from that the tour guides proffered. If you know students who go to a specific school you are visiting, make sure to meet them and ask them about their experiences. In particular, make sure to visit their dorm rooms and their dorm in general. Look at the common space, look at the dorm room, meet his/her roommate/s and friends and try to imagine yourself there. Can you? If you can, make sure that schools stays in the running.

THE WINNING ATTITUDE

Now, at the end of high school, there are a few areas that will demonstrate the winning attitude. If you act and think accordingly, it means that you have successfully embraced the high school experience and the application process. It also means that you are ready to embrace the many challenges of life.

Do you want to be a winner?

Of course, all of us want to be winners! But why are only some of us winners? It is because winning requires persistence, work, and vision. The winning attitude, in my opinion, is first most exemplified in life at the end of high school when most students get senioritis.

First let us look at how Students A and B would look at the end of senior year.

Student A: Senior year is the time to use my experience and my know-how to win competitions. This is the time to work harder actually, but I can also relax too. I will apply to the most competitions this year and maintain good grades.

Student B: Man, let us just relax. We have been working hard for so long, it is time just to sit back and let the results come in. We have finished that dreadful, horrifying, and boring application process. Maybe my grades will slide a little, but really who cares? I mean, I already sent in my

As you can imagine, many students follow Student B and lose **focus**. The winning attitude, as you can tell, is that of Student A. He/she accepts more work and goes forward with a can-do attitude. It is at the end of the race, at the end of high school, where true champions are found. Continuing with your passion because you *love* it is the true test of persistence. It is at this end of the race where I began seeing this attitude so clearly—and astonishingly I found the results of my friends to be correlated to their attitude toward senior year.

It is this attitude of persistence that is the epitome of success. It is what will ultimately separate those who get into many top schools from those who do not. It will separate those who are very successful in life from those who are not. It is that **self-drive**. At the beginning of this book, I spoke about *embracing* the process. I tell you a bigger aspect of life here: **self-drive**. This is that inner passion for what you do. I honestly believe that it all starts in 9th grade, if not earlier. The earlier you learn to have passion for what you do, I think the better. This is why the application process is necessary and beautiful. It is a measure of passion. Admissions officers seek passionate individuals who can dedicate themselves to a task, whether it be a test, a dance, or a performance, and do it in entirety. Shoot for the stars. Work towards your goals. Good luck and enjoy the experience.

Remember that whatever the admission decisions may be, that they occurred for the best. Admissions officers look for the best "fits" for their particular schools, but in doing so, they also, by nature, simultaneously look for the best "fit" for you! Looking back on my admissions process, I found that the schools I was not accepted to were not fit for me and I was not fit for them. Know that what happens is for the best. And if you are still not happy with the results, know that nothing is set in stone. The process is "human" — humans read your application. You can always petition. But even greater than a petition is knowing that you can be whatever you want, you can do whatever you want, if you want to do it badly enough. There is no limit in the real world and do not let college bind you. It is a time to learn, grow, experience, and develop, but that often occurs through informal interactions outside of the classroom that are usually not considered part of the stereotypical college experience: large lecture rooms and complex equations on chalkboards. Go for the world, it is waiting for you. Show your passion in as many ways as you can, the time is yours, now and always.

TIPS, TRICKS, AND WEBSITES

As some of you might feel, this book can sometimes be vague. Its purpose is to give you *insight* from a previous, relatively successful applicant and his experiences through the process: what to do, what to avoid, and how to spend your precious time. Successful people view time as an asset, something that we can utilize in a positive way, whereas others see it as a limiting factor. Using it in the right way is key to successful decisions and meaningful practice of success.

As for the some of the specifics of the application process, such as when to take the SAT (which month is the best), or exactly what theme to choose for your application, I leave that to you because it is *individualized*. If I tell you what to do, then you are not writing about yourself, you are writing about me! And that defeats the entire purpose of the college admissions process: to have a meaningful, deep, multifaceted conversation about who you are, what your dreams are, and what you have done to show that to an admissions officer, another human being with experience and expertise.

For specifics, I recommend you develop your *personalized* approach to the process by gaining all that you can about common approaches and by reading books like these. I will offer you some general sources here that I used to develop this personalized approach to the specifics of the admission process.

1. College Confidential/College Discussion
   http://talk.collegeconfidential.com/

WHAT TO DO: This is a *deep* resource that is especially useful for the conglomerate wisdom that students put together. Look at how students faired (often students post SAT scores, GPA, and extracurricular activities to get judged about their chances) and then see how they actually faired. This historical slate is invaluable. Read through the top threads about what to do, extracurricular activity advice and so forth.

WHAT TO WATCH OUT FOR: BEWARE—this is the site where many myths in this book originated from. Some misinformed parents and students post on here, so do not believe everything you read, although often others correct wrong information,

2. Case Studies

This last category of references is something unique that I found very valuable. I think that many successful individuals have mentors, and I think they provide a source of inspiration. During my high school years I followed many students who were either one or two years older than me (often successful scientists because that was my field). Follow role models, see what they do, how they fare in the admission process, and try to see why they were successful. Having tangible dreams can make your dreams become reality.

Some useful websites:

<u>National Association for College Admission Counseling</u>

> http://www.nacacnet.org/PUBLICATIONSRESOURCES/Pages/default.aspx *WHAT TO DO:* This site has a general roadmap of what you should expect from your four years of high school and how you should plan for these years. Generally, this is accurate and what many school counselors will also tell you. Some other aspects of the site, such as the flowchart with elements that colleges consider, are also valuable for perspective.

PART 7: RESOURCES

THE COMMON APPLICATION

Below is the Common Application, a series of documents that are sent to most schools you apply to. The Common Application has merged with all of the Ivy League Schools and most other schools. Some schools, like the UC system, have remained off of the Common Application, however.

The first two pages of the Common Application are purely informational and are designed to match the application to the person who is applying. Fill out the information, and do not stress too much about "Academic Interests" or "Career Interest". Most admissions officers know that students change their mind often and won't read too deeply into these inputs.

2011-12 FIRST-YEAR APPLICATION
For Spring 2012 or Fall 2012 Enrollment

APPLICANT

Legal Name S _____ A _____
Last/Family/Sur (Enter name exactly as it appears on official documents.) First/Given   Middle (complete)   Jr., etc.

Preferred name, if not first name (only one) _____   Former last name(s) _____

Birth Date ___12/12/1932___ ○ Female ☑ Male   US Social Security Number, if any _____
mm/dd/yyyy   Required for US Citizens and Permanent Residents applying for financial aid via FAFSA

Preferred Telephone ○ Home ○ Cell Home (_123_) 123-1234 _____ Cell (____)_____
Area/Country/City Code   Area/Country/City Code

E-mail Address as@gmail.com _____   IM Address _____

Permanent home address 123 Albany Way _____
Number & Street   Apartment #

Yorktown _____   NY United States of America   12345
City/Town   County or Parish   State/Province   Country   ZIP/Postal Code

If different from above, please give your current mailing address for all admission correspondence.   (from _____ to _____
mm/dd/yyyy   mm/dd/yyyy

Current mailing address _____
Number & Street   Apartment #

_____   _____
City/Town   County or Parish   State/Province   Country   ZIP/Postal Code

If your current mailing address is a boarding school, include name of school here: _____

FUTURE PLANS

Your answers to these questions will vary for different colleges. If the online system did not ask you to answer some of the questions you see in this section, this college chose not to ask that question of its applicants.

College _____   Deadline _____
mm/dd/yyyy

Entry Term: ○ Fall (Jul-Dec) ○ Spring (Jan-Jun)   Do you intend to apply for need-based financial aid? ○ Yes ○ No
Decision Plan_____   Do you intend to apply for merit-based scholarships? ○ Yes ○ No
Academic Interests _____   Do you intend to be a full-time student? ○ Yes ○ No
_____   Do you intend to enroll in a degree program your first year? ○ Yes ○ No
_____   Do you intend to live in college housing? _____
Career Interest_____   What is the highest degree you intend to earn? _____

DEMOGRAPHICS

Citizenship Status _____   1. Are you Hispanic/Latino?
Non-US Citizenship _____   ○ Yes, Hispanic or Latino (including Spain) ○ No If yes, please describe your background
_____
_____   2. Regardless of your answer to the prior question, please indicate how you identify
_____   yourself. (Check one or more and describe your background.)
Birthplace _____   ○ American Indian or Alaska Native (including all Original Peoples of the Americas)
City/Town   State/Province   Country
Years lived in the US? _____ Years lived outside the US? _____   Are you Enrolled? ○ Yes ○ No If yes, please enter Tribal Enrollment Number_____

Language Proficiency (Check all that apply.)
S(Speak) R(Read) W(Write) F(First Language) H(Spoken at Home)   S R W F H   ○ Asian (including Indian subcontinent and Philippines)
_____   ○ ○ ○ ○ ○
_____   ○ ○ ○ ○ ○   ○ Black or African American (including Africa and Caribbean)
_____   ○ ○ ○ ○ ○
   ○ Native Hawaiian or Other Pacific Islander (Original Peoples)
Optional The items with a gray background are optional. No information you
provide will be used in a discriminatory manner.
Religious Preference _____   ○ White (including Middle Eastern)

US Armed Services veteran status _____

8887452   A S   Generated Online AP-1/2011

1

The section "Family" can have an impact on your application, because of affirmative action. Also, if you parents are alumni of a university it can have a positive effect on your application. Having a brother or sister attend the university you are applying to can make a positive difference, but generally it is considered to be not as much as having a parent alumni.

FAMILY

Please list both parents below, even if one or more is deceased or no longer has legal responsibilities toward you. Many colleges collect this information for demographic purposes even if you are an adult or an emancipated minor. If you are a minor with a legal guardian (an individual or government entity), then please list that information below as well. If you wish, you may list step-parents and/or other adults with whom you reside, or who otherwise care for you, in the Additional Information section.

Household

Parents' marital status (relative to each other): ○ Never Married ○ Married ○ Civil Union/Domestic Partners ○ Widowed ○ Separated ○ Divorced (date _____)

With whom do you make your permanent home? ○ Parent 1 ○ Parent 2 ○ Both ○ Legal Guardian ○ Ward of the Court/State ○ Other

If you have children, how many? _____

Parent 1: ○ Mother ○ Father ○ Unknown

Is Parent 1 living? ○ Yes ○ No (Date Deceased _____)
mm/yyyy

_____
Last/Family/Sur   First/Given   Middle   Title (Mr./Mrs./Ms./Dr.)

Country of birth _____

Home address if different from yours

_____

_____

Preferred Telephone: ○ Home ○ Cell ○ Work (_____) _____
Area/Country/City Code

E-mail _____

Occupation _____

Employer _____

College (if any) _____ CEEB _____

Degree _____ Year _____

Graduate School (if any) _____ CEEB _____

Degree _____ Year _____

Parent 2: ○ Mother ○ Father ○ Unknown

Is Parent 2 living? ○ Yes ○ No (Date Deceased _____)
mm/yyyy

_____
Last/Family/Sur   First/Given   Middle   Title (Mr./Mrs./Ms./Dr.)

Country of birth _____

Home address if different from yours

_____

_____

Preferred Telephone: ○ Home ○ Cell ○ Work (_____) _____
Area/Country/City Code

E-mail _____

Occupation _____

Employer _____

College (if any) _____ CEEB _____

Degree _____ Year _____

Graduate School (if any) _____ CEEB _____

Degree _____ Year _____

Legal Guardian *(if other than a parent)*

Relationship to you _____

_____
Last/Family/Sur   First/Given   Middle   Title (Mr./Mrs./Ms./Dr.)

Country of birth _____

Home address if different from yours

_____

_____

Preferred Telephone: ○ Home ○ Cell ○ Work (_____) _____
Area/Country/City Code

E-mail _____

Occupation _____

Employer _____

College (if any) _____ CEEB _____

Degree _____ Year _____

Graduate School (if any) _____ CEEB _____

Degree _____ Year _____

Siblings

Please give names and ages of your brothers or sisters. If they are enrolled in grades K-12 (or international equivalent), list their grade levels. If they have attended or are currently attending college, give the names of the undergraduate institution, degree earned, and approximate dates of attendance. If more than three siblings, please list them in the Additional Information section.

Name	Age & Grade	Relationship

College Attended _____ CEEB _____

Degree earned or expected _____ Dates _____
mm/yyyy – mm/yyyy

Name	Age & Grade	Relationship

College Attended _____ CEEB _____

Degree earned or expected _____ Dates _____
mm/yyyy – mm/yyyy

Name	Age & Grade	Relationship

College Attended _____ CEEB _____

Degree earned or expected _____ Dates _____
mm/yyyy – mm/yyyy

EDUCATION

Secondary Schools

Most recent secondary school attended _____

Entry Date _____ Graduation Date _____ School Type: ○ Public ○ Charter ○ Independent ○ Religious ○ Home School
  mm/yyyy   *mm/dd/yyyy*

Address _____ CEEB/ACT Code _____
  Number & Street

_____
City/Town   *State/Province*   *Country*   *ZIP/Postal Code*

Counselor's Name _____ Counselor's Title _____

E-mail _____ Telephone (_____)_____ Fax (_____)_____
                              Area/Country/City Code   Number   Ext.   *Area/Country/City Code   Number*

List all other secondary schools you have attended since 9th grade, including summer schools or enrichment programs hosted on a secondary school campus:

School Name & CEEB/ACT Code	Location (City, State/Province, ZIP/Postal Code, Country)	Dates Attended (mm/yyyy)

Please list any community program/organization that has provided free assistance with your application process: _____

If your education was or will be interrupted, please indicate so here and provide details in the Additional Information section: _____

Colleges & Universities Report all college attendance (including online) since 9th grade and indicate as College Course (CO) or Enrichment Program (EP) hosted on a college campus.

College/University Name & CEEB/ACT Code	Location (City, State/Province, ZIP/Postal Code, Country)	Degree Candidate? Yes	CO	EP	Dates Attended mm/yyyy – mm/yyyy	Degree Earned
		○	○	○		
		○	○	○		
		○	○	○		

Were you issued a transcript for any work listed above? ○ Yes ○ No   If yes, please have an official transcript sent as soon as possible.

ACADEMICS

The self-reported information in this section is not intended to take the place of your official records. Please note the requirements of each institution to which you are applying and arrange for official transcripts and score reports to be sent from your secondary school and the appropriate testing agencies. Where "Best Scores" are requested, please report the highest individual scores you have earned so far, even if those scores are from different test dates.

Grades _____ Class Rank _____ Class Size _____ Weighted? ○ Yes ○ No   GPA _____ Scale _____ Weighted? ○ Yes ○ No
            (if available)   *(if available)*

ACT Exam Dates: _____ _____ _____   Best Scores: _____
     (past & future) *mm/yyyy mm/yyyy mm/yyyy*   *(so far)*

	COMP	mm/yyyy	English	mm/yyyy	Math	mm/yyyy
	Reading	mm/yyyy	Science	mm/yyyy	Writing	mm/yyyy

SAT Exam Dates: _____ _____ _____   Best Scores: _____
     (past & future) *mm/yyyy mm/yyyy mm/yyyy*   *(so far)*

	Critical Reading	mm/yyyy	Math	mm/yyyy	Writing	mm/yyyy

TOEFL/ Exam Dates: _____ _____ _____   Best Score: _____
IELTS *(past & future)* *mm/yyyy mm/yyyy mm/yyyy*   *(so far)*

	Test	Score	mm/yyyy

AP/IB/SAT Best Scores: _____
Subjects *(per subject, so far)* *mm/yyyy*

Type & Subject	Score	mm/yyyy	Type & Subject	Score
mm/yyyy Type & Subject	Score	*mm/yyyy*	Type & Subject	Score
mm/yyyy Type & Subject	Score	*mm/yyyy*	Type & Subject	Score
mm/yyyy Type & Subject	Score	*mm/yyyy*	Type & Subject	Score

Current Courses Please indicate title, level (AP, IB, advanced honors, etc.) and credit value of all courses you are taking this year. Indicate quarter classes taken in the same semester on the appropriate semester line.

Full Year/First Semester/First Trimester	Second Semester/Trimester	Third Trimester *or additional first/second term courses if more space is needed*

Now comes the important part of the Common Application. The reason why this book has emphasized so heavily looking carefully into extracurricular activities is because every second of our time here should be used wisely, but also because of this page. Activities need to visibly demonstrate an end—that is how the human mind puts values on things. Activities hopefully result in awards or some kind of distinction that can be put on the Honors column. At the same time, not having an International level of achievement is not a dream-crusher. Sometimes, family is an important part of who we are and that cannot be shown on this page. Instead, it should be evident in your essays. Deciding what to put down in the" Extracurricular Activities & Work Experience" is crucial, and should be listed always in the order of importance, with the most important at the top. Often, if you have done many activities in high school, all of them will not fit on this page. Choose the most important ones.

Honors Briefly list any academic distinctions or honors you have received since the 9th grade or international equivalent (e.g., National Merit, Cum Laude Society).
S(School) S/R(State or Regional) N(National) I(International)

Grade level or post-graduate (PG) 9 10 11 12 PG	Honor	Highest Level Recognition S S/R N
○○○○○ _____		○○○
○○○○○ _____		○○○
○○○○○ _____		○○○
○○○○○ _____		○○○
○○○○○ _____		○○○

EXTRACURRICULAR ACTIVITIES & WORK EXPERIENCE

Extracurricular Please list your **principal** extracurricular, volunteer, and work activities **in their order of importance to you.** Feel free to group your activities paid work experience separately if you prefer. Use the space available to provide details of your activities and accomplishments (specific events, varsity letter, mus instrument, employer, etc.). **To allow us to focus on the highlights of your activities, please complete this section even if you plan to attach a résumé.**

Grade level or post-graduate (PG) 9 10 11 12 PG	Approximate time spent — Hours per week / Weeks per year	When did you participate in the activity? School year / Summer/ School Break	Position held, honors won, letters earned, or employer	If applicable do you p to particip in colleg
○○○○○ ____ ____	○ ○	_____	○
Activity _____			
○○○○○ ____ ____	○ ○	_____	○
Activity _____			
○○○○○ ____ ____	○ ○	_____	○
Activity _____			
○○○○○ ____ ____	○ ○	_____	○
Activity _____			
○○○○○ ____ ____	○ ○	_____	○
Activity _____			
○○○○○ ____ ____	○ ○	_____	○
Activity _____			
○○○○○ ____ ____	○ ○	_____	○
Activity _____			
○○○○○ ____ ____	○ ○	_____	○
Activity _____			
○○○○○ ____ ____	○ ○	_____	○
Activity _____			
○○○○○ ____ ____	○ ○	_____	○
Activity _____			

In this next page, there is the short essay response. You can answer any way you like, choosing a particular prompt will not give you an advantage. For prompt 1, choose an activity that you do not highlight later on in the longer essays to add diversity to your application and show your breadth. In the longer essays, you will have a chance to expound on a significant experience deeply, so you do not need to briefly brush over it here. Being succinct and to-the-point is key for this part of the Application.

WRITING

Please briefly elaborate on one of your extracurricular activities or work experiences in the space below.

Please write an essay of 250 – 500 words on a topic of your choice or on one of the options listed below, and attach it to your application before submission. **Please indicate your topic by checking the appropriate box.** This personal essay helps us become acquainted with you as a person and student, apart from courses, grades, test scores, and other objective data. It will also demonstrate your ability to organize your thoughts and express yourself. *NOTE: Your Common Application essay should be the same for all colleges. Do not customize it in any way for individual colleges. Colleges that want customized essay responses will ask for them on a supplement form.*

- **1** Evaluate a significant experience, achievement, risk you have taken, or ethical dilemma you have faced and its impact on you.
- **2** Discuss some issue of personal, local, national, or international concern and its importance to you.
- **3** Indicate a person who has had a significant influence on you, and describe that influence.
- **4** Describe a character in fiction, a historical figure, or a creative work (as in art, music, science, etc.) that has had an influence on you, and explain that influence.
- **5** A range of academic interests, personal perspectives, and life experiences adds much to the educational mix. Given your personal background, describe an experience that illustrates what you would bring to the diversity in a college community or an encounter that demonstrated the importance of diversity to you.
- **6** Topic of your choice.

Additional Information Please attach a separate sheet if you wish to provide details of circumstances or qualifications not reflected in the application.

Disciplinary History

◯ Have you ever been found responsible for a disciplinary violation at any educational institution you have attended from the 9ᵗʰ grade (or the international equivalent) forward, whether related to academic misconduct or behavioral misconduct, that resulted in a disciplinary action? These actions could include, but are not limited to: probation, suspension, removal, dismissal, or expulsion from the institution. ◯ Yes ◯ No

◯ Have you ever been adjudicated guilty or convicted of a misdemeanor, felony, or other crime? ◯ Yes ◯ No
[Note that you are not required to answer "yes" to this question, or provide an explanation, if the criminal adjudication or conviction has been expunged, sealed, annulled, pardoned, destroyed, erased, impounded, or otherwise ordered by a court to be kept confidential.]

If you answered "yes" to either or both questions, please attach a separate sheet of paper that gives the approximate date of each incident, explains the circumstances, and reflects on what you learned from the experience.

Note: Applicants are expected to immediately notify the institutions to which they are applying should there be any changes to the information requested on this application, including disciplinary history.

SIGNATURE

Application Fee Payment If this college requires an application fee, how will you be paying it?

◯ Online Payment   ◯ Will Mail Payment   ◯ Online Fee Waiver Request   ◯ Will Mail Fee Waiver Request

Required Signature

☐ I certify that all information submitted in the admission process—including the application, the personal essay, any supplements, and any other supporting materials—is my own work, factually true, and honestly presented, and that these documents will become the property of the institutions to which I am applying and will not be returned to me. I understand that I may be subject to a range of possible disciplinary actions, including admission revocation, expulsion, or revocation of course credit, grades, and degree, should the information I have certified be false.

☐ I acknowledge that I have reviewed the application instructions for each college receiving this application. I understand that all offers of admission are conditional, pending receipt of final transcripts showing work comparable in quality to that upon which the offer was based, as well as honorable dismissal from the school.

☐ I affirm that I will send an enrollment deposit (or equivalent) to only one institution; sending multiple deposits (or equivalent) may result in the withdrawal of my admission offers from all institutions. [Note: Students may send an enrollment deposit (or equivalent) to a second institution where they have been admitted from the waitlist, provided that they inform the first institution that they will no longer be enrolling.]

Signature _____   Date _____
                                                                                                     mm/dd/yyyy

Common Application member institution admission offices do not discriminate on the basis of race, color, ethnicity, national origin, religion, creed, sex, age, marital status, parental status, physical disability, learning disability, political affiliation, veteran status, or sexual orientation.

Now comes a very critical part, the Supplements. For every school you apply to through the Common Application, you will need to submit a Supplement, which generally contains a few essays or short responses and asks you to identify why you want to attend a particular university and other similar questions. Some universities have further background information to be inputted on their Supplements and no essays, but most have at least one essay prompt.

When Supplements give the option of a non-required essay, I recommend students to always complete this essay with something new about themselves or something they think they have not told the college yet. Why not take the chance to talk more to an admissions officer, continuing a conversation further so they understand you more fully?

HELPFUL WEBSITES

The more independent research you do, the better prepared you are for the admissions process. Try to visit websites to get a general feel of the process.

Assorted helpful websites:

www.edwise.com
www.ibringo.org
www.fastweb.com
http://www.usnews.com/topics/subjects/college_admissions
www.collegeboard.com
http://www.honestcollege.com/
www.collegesavings.org
www.college-scholarships.com
www.scholarships.fatomei.com/index.html
https://www.commonapp.org/CommonApp/default.aspx
www.scholarships.com
http://blogs.makingitcount.com/yearone/
http://www.csssa.org/
http://www.eduwonk.com/
http://www.uwyo.edu/hsi/

http://www.collegeconfidential.com/college_admissions/

http://money.howstuffworks.com/personal-finance/college-planning/admissions/colle
admission.htm

http://thechoice.blogs.nytimes.com/

www.students.gov

www.casac.ca.gov

http://www.collegeparents.org/

www.fasfa.gov

http://www.summer.harvard.edu/programs/ssp/default.jsp

http://collegesearch.collegeboard.com/search/index.jsp

www.studentloans.gov

http://collegetipsforparents.org/

www.studentscholarship.org

http://www.college.gov/wps/portal

http://collegeapps.about.com/

http://youthprograms.mtu.edu/

COMPETITIONS

Writing	Arts	Science
• Ayn Rand Essay Contest	• New York Conservatory for Dramatic Arts Scholarships	• Local (County) Science Fair
• MathMovesU	• Irene Ryan Acting Scholarships	• State Science Fair
• TeenInk Poetry/Fiction Contests	• Camera USA: National Photography Award	• Science Bowl
• Penguin.com Essay Contest	• Young Arts Foundation	• Science Olympiad
• Growing up Asian in America Art and Essay Contest	• St. Augustine Art Association International Fine Art Exhibition	• USABO, USACO, USAMO (and respective international competitions such as IMO)
• ALBA George Watt Memorial Essay Contest		• MathMovesU Essay Contest
• FRA Americanism Essay Contest		• University Poster Presentations

GLOSSARY OF KEY TERMS

A

Academic tests — Tests that are used to measure academic potential, **focus**, ability, and applicant character. These tests are the SAT (Standardized Aptitude Test), ACT, and the SAT subject tests. Although critical to admissions officers' perspective on an applicant's academic initiative, they are not the only factor considered, and one should not give myopic focus to these few elements.

Activity document — A document that helps students organize their activities into scope (local, regional, state, and national) and into thematic threads by highlighting activities that go together.

"Adcom" — An acronym for "admissions committee" that is often used on forums and online blogs such as College Discussion.

Application-supplement packets — These packets are standardized packets containing hard copies of your supplementary materials with a cover letter which briefly explains what is included and further identification information. These packets are sent to every college you apply to.

Areas of concentration — This area is the general area which you decide to focus in on and eventually your **theme** will somehow be associated with this general field. This area is correlated to your **niche** as well.

Arts document — A document that contains all of the readings that students do during the required 30 minutes a week outside of class, whether it be books, blogs, or anything similar. This document also contains interesting movies, music or anything related to the arts that students enjoy.

B

Bar-setting tests — Tests that are meant to differentiate students based on basic skills such as the ability to speak English. The prime example is the TOEFL. Although used in the admissions process, my international classmates suggest that one should focus on **academic tests** such as the SAT and ACT that are more heavily used to determine applicant character and ability.

Benchmark faculty members — These are faculty members who make specific departments famous at certain institutions. They are the ones that teach classes that students praise and ones that become many students' favorite class.

"Big Thing" — This is your biggest achievement or biggest extracurricular activity that defines your **theme** and most of your extracurricular activities. It helps you write your **one-sentence** and helps admissions officers grasp who you are, your dedication to a particular field, and your vision. Often, this thing is what differentiates acceptances and rejects from top schools.

"Big thing" myth — There is a common misconception that a **"big thing"** is necessary to gaining acceptance to top colleges. This is not true, it is not mandatory — however, in many cases, especially in the academic niche, it is almost necessary.

Boxing — Individuals get "boxed" into certain categories based on factors such as ethnicity, course load, extracurricular activity, and personality. I highly discourage boxing yourself or others around you because it goes against the very notion of the application process of discovering your individuality and your purpose.

C

Choice list of schools — The list of schools that you apply to, in order of preference. I highly discourage students from creating this kind of list or from even developing preferences. Please read Dream School Predicament and School-Centric Approach for more information.

Competition-centric approach — In activity-building and resume building, consider taking this approach. In this approach, the student applies to many competitions in the hopes of winning an award or gaining an achievement that can succinctly be described on a resume, can contribute to his/her **one-sentence, theme,** and demonstrate passion. Often, in this approach, a **"big thing"** can be developed by applying to many competitions and hopefully winning one or more than one.

Consistent practice — This is the centerpiece to success on standardized exams. The regiment I recommend is simulating entire exams, practice exams, once a week until test week. This way, students get to practice content, form, and timing at once.

Constructive realist — Knowing where you stand (whether it be in reference to your ability to gain admission to certain colleges or how you are performing on practice tests) but also being constructive about this stance. Know that you can always improve and what to expect.

Content-focused approach — This describes a strategy for choosing which SAT Subject tests to take. In this approach, students take Subject tests in related areas to demonstrate a mastery of particular content.

Cover page — The first page of the **red-yellow-green** method that is placed in front of all other materials in the packet created for each school, including average GPA and SAT scores and some unique aspects of each school.

Critical eye — Reading information, especially information on the Internet, about college admissions or even statistics that can be misleading, with a realistic mindset. Know that statistics can be inflated or misrepresenting information (refer to *How to Lie with Statistics*) and also that misinformed parents, "trolls" (people who post wrong information on purpose), or misinformed students can post online. At the same time, know that there is so much experience and valuable information on the Internet that can give you great insight into the entire process. College Discussion gave me years and years of historical records of student portfolios and results that are invaluable, for instance, and I attribute the Internet as one of the greatest sources for developing my own opinion of this entire process.

D

Demonstrated need — This is a buzzword used in financial aid offices to describe a student who has shown the need for aid, whether it be loans or grants, through FASFA/CSS forms, W-2 forms, or similar documentation.

Dependent — This term is used in financial aid to describe a student who usually has one or more the following characteristics and must use parents' income in CSS/FASFA forms and in evaluation of demonstrated need : under 24 years old, no children or dependents, not married, not a veteran, not a graduate or professional degree seeking student, and not a ward of the court.

Dispersed approach — This method of essay writing occurs when students write parts of essays at a time, maybe even complete drafts of some essays, but spread their focus over a number of essays. This method is recommended because it gives students a mental "break" from certain types of prompts and spurs creativity.

Diversity approach — In this approach, students take SAT Subject tests in a range of areas to exhibit mastery in all of these areas. Often, student without a predefined strength such as math, science, or English will take this approach.

Dream school predicament — This term describes the problems with getting emotionally attached to one school or a set of schools before admissions. The Dream School Predicament describes how to avoid this problem.

E

Essay fatigue — Tiredness resulting from long writing stretches or a general tiredness from writing, which usually occurs near the end of the application process. To avoid this tiredness, try taking short strategic breaks and convincing yourself the value of what you are doing and the short time you have to convey yourself to someone else.

F

Facilitated reading — Physically reading with your child in order to encourage them, parents use this method and read their own material while a child (often in the 5th-8th grade) reads what they enjoy in a structured fashion at least once a week for 30 minutes.

Focus — Perhaps the most important of the three skills developed in high school, this skill refers to the ability to concentrate on a particular task and complete it well. The average level to which an activity is completed refers to the quality of a student's work and is judged in the application process in the form of GPA, or Grade Point Average.

> **Constant focus** — This is a higher level of focus which the student gains after many, many repetitions of consciously focusing on a task. When switching between tasks, the student is able to maintain concentration and can tune out distractions. There is no break of concentration.

Focused approach—This method of essay approach allows students to write one essay at time, completing one before moving onto the next. However, this method can often lead to the **dream school predicament** or be a result of that problem, and is not recommended.

Free write—Writing without stopping and about anything—focusing on developing creativity and working towards writing the admissions essay.

G

"Grace period"—The time that students have to pay back loans, a term usually used for repayment of federal loans.

Grammar readers—These are individuals who read your essays, skimming over content, in search for grammar errors.

H

High-output approach—Students apply to many schools in many different geographic locations and with different prestige in the hopes of increasing their possible choices once decisions come out. I recommend this approach to most students because it usually gives students more flexibility and more freedom in applying to more schools. The only downside is more work—which can easily be done.

"Hit"—The phenomenon when an admission officer happens to "click" with something you said in you essay or in any part of your application. It could be that he/she participated in the same activity or thought the same way about something. The more hits, the better.

I

Ideal admissions officer — Namely, this is the first part of identifying yourself and the first part of your essay process. Imagining this person and what he/she would be like will help you discover yourself. The complete description is in An Introduction to the Essay.

Independent — This term is used in financial aid to describe a student who usually has one or more of the following characteristics, and can use his/her income level to determine loans or demonstrated need: over 24 years old, children or dependents, married, a veteran, a graduate or professional degree seeking student, and a ward of the court.

Interview packets — These are hard copy packets of your supplementary materials and your resume that you standardize and take to every interview to give to the interviewer.

"In range" schools — These schools are competitive schools that the student thinks they have a fair chance of getting admitted to.

I-statements — These thoughts are usually structured beginning with "I" and referencing a direct verb, to make concise and simple personal statements, such as "I enjoy reading".

L

Linear applicant—The applicant that believes that college leads to a job, and that is the sole goal and motivation of college. These kinds of applicants are often rejected and wonder why they are not successful.

Low-output approach—Students apply to very few schools because they have a strong desire to attend only a select few schools or a certain type of school. I highly discourage students from taking this approach, please refer to The School-Centric Approach for more information.

M

Medium-output approach—Students apply to several schools but definitely not the number that they could apply to. Students are more selective in this approach, but they still do allow themselves diversification and backup institutions.

Merit-based—This type of grant is dependent on some kind of metric, such as an essay or application, that determines a student is eligible for some award.

N

Need-based—This type of loan or grant is dependent on whether schools or officials see a demonstrated need for financial aid, determined through income statements and CSS/FASFA forms

Niche — This a loosely used term to define the "area" that students fall under: athletic, academic, or legacy are the three most commonly accepted niches.

Number one school — This refers to the common notion that many students have (especially those aiming at top schools) about having a first choice institution. I highly advise students against having this school in mind, please refer to Dream School Predicament for more information.

Notification submission — This is a document, recording, or some other record of an achievement that the student gained after submitting the application and supplementary materials. It is usually achieved in January and sent in that same month.

O

One-sentence approach — In this approach, the individual polishes their **theme** and their **specificity hook** by trying to describe their extracurricular involvements in one sentence. It could also be manipulated to include the student's **"big thing"**.

Out-of-application supplementary materials — These materials are those which are submitted outside of any application, including independent research or musical recordings. They help demonstrate a **"big thing"** and a passion, but applicants must be careful about exactly what they submit, including their Common App ID and following the detailed specifications schools usually provide.

P

Personal response: The essay written in response to a purely "creative prompt", an essay completely about the self and written with the **personal writing** method.

Personal Writing — Exposition that focuses on your emotions, your beliefs, and your thought processes.

Perspective — The ability to add individuality to a scenario, class, or other event from personal experience, outlook on life, and upbringing. Often, perspective is determined by subjective elements of the application, and primarily by the essays. The essay is a reflection of who you are and how you think, which is fundamentally shaped by your perspective.

Presentation — The cohesive "finish" that your complete application, your supplementary materials, and your interview present to everyone who judges you (admissions officers, professors reading your supplementary materials, and interviewers).

Personalized approach — You develop your own approach to test taking, no matter if you have had much experience with test tutors or have done all of your studying alone. If you study with tutors, it is often either a mixture of your tutor's methods and your own approach. The only way to develop this approach is to do practice tests and learn the way you approach the questions. The way you approach the test and understand its questions, even if it is standardized, affects the way you answer the questions. Remember to give yourself time to develop your own approach — it took me two years.

Perspective Approach—A method discussed through the admissions process in this book for developing an understanding of why we do an activity, such as writing essays, in conjugation with how we do these activities. Combining understanding with action, this method gives meaning and power and is applicable to any part of life. Its goal is to build strong and moral minds and through that end people that are successful in both college admissions and in life.

Prioritization—The second of the big skills developed in high school, this skill refers to the ability to differentiate between the value of various extracurricular activities, classes, and relaxation and gauge what should be more important and what should be less important.

> **Tunneling process**—This process refers to the tunneling, or choosing, between options in the world. For some, we are faced with options starting in middle school when there are dozens of school clubs to join. For others, this begins in high school. In any case it is closely tied prioritizing your time and the fast you learn how to tunnel, the more effective you can be in the organizations you choose.

R

"Reach" schools—These are schools with exceptionally low acceptance rates and are usually affiliated with certain designations (Ivy League) or have a reputation of excellence and great prestige. They often draw some of the smartest students from around the globe.

Resume-builder — This is an electronic document in which you record every activity, award, or event you were invited to attend or attended that you think could be part of your resume. I encourage you to start this document as early as possible (the beginning of 9th grade at latest).

"Resume pad" — A tactic that is used by some students in which they do activities, especially work experience internships or jobs, for the purpose of filling a resume or trying to show that they have learned valuable skills such as the value of money. This word is often used in a negative light. Instead of focusing on filling your resume, instead focusing on finding what you love and then doing that, honestly and genuinely.

Reviewing block — This block is caused by reviewing your essays so much that you start to edit and think in the same way you were before. Or alternatively you cannot stand editing your essay anymore and do not want to. When you feel a block coming on, make sure to take a break by doing something different for a while, then start again.

S

"Safety" schools — These are schools that students think they have an exceptional chance of being accepted too and are often considered "backups" to worst case admissions results. Still, they do not have 100 percent acceptance rates.

School-centric approach — In this approach, students apply to schools which they *honestly* can envision themselves at for the next four years of their lives.

Scope—The ability to scale up your extracurricular activity from a local to a state, nation, or internationally-recognized organization. Choose organizations to join based on this trait.

Self-drive—This is the singular most important concept in this text, referring to the drive that a student develops after embracing a task. In the last chapter of this text, I extend this embrace from the embrace of the application process to any task in life and to the drive that follows.

Shotgun approach—In this approach, students are exposed to a variety of academic fields or extracurricular activities. This term is used in two contexts: parents expose younger students (1st-5th grade) to different areas through active involvement or students expose themselves to different fields (usually beginning in 6th grade).

Shotgun-local method—This method of choosing which scholarships to apply for involves applying for most local scholarships that a student can find with relatively low monetary returns.

Simulation—This is a thought experiment that I encourage students to do several times in the admissions process in which students imagine themselves physically at a university. They are to imagine what the atmosphere is like and how they thrive in that environment.

Specificity—The level of detail that you go through the entire application process will determine the quality and substantive nature of your extracurricular activities, your **theme**, your **one sentence**, your essays, your standardized scores, and your interview. Being detail-oriented is critical to this entire process.

Specificity Hook — A hook is anything that is unique to you. This hook falls under your **theme** and is usually your **"big thing"** if you have one. This particular hook refers to the specific nature of your work that allows you to show so much passion and dedication to a field that you have focused in on a particular area that interests you.

T

Target-national method — In this approach, students apply to larger, prestigious scholarships and put more effort into these high-return endeavors.

Theme — This is the most important part of your extracurricular application and of your non-academic aspect as presented in the application. Your central area of focus, which weaves through everything that you have done, will be the factor that differentiates you from other applicants and is often the factor that differentiates admissions in top schools.

The One-Test Wonder myth — There is the common misconception that there are individuals who can ace standardized examinations without any practice. Although statistically I cannot say that they do not exist, I have never met such an individual nor have any of my contemporaries. Do not believe that you are this individual, and even if you are, hard work never goes to waste and will solidify your thinking process.

Thinking period — This the period that students afford themselves when they start the admission process earlier. They get more time to think about themselves and usually produce higher quality overall applications.

Thread — An aspect of your complete written application. The more threads, the better.

Three-tier method — This classic strategy for choosing which schools to apply to is one that I also recommend. In this strategy, students apply to three "tiers" of schools with the hopes of being admitted to some in each category.

Time bubble — The limited space that students often "cram" essay writing for colleges in — usually the last two weeks of December before the December 31st deadline.

Time-centric approach — This approach follows an earlier, stricter timeline of writing college essays but also allows the student more time to edit. In this approach time is abundant and students capitalize on the extra time by using it to edit and polish their essays.

Time management — Using time in your favor is one of the most useful skills that should be learned in high school, particularly. Learning time management can start earlier, however.

> **Time-oriented management** — Division and production is tallied by time instead of task. In this approach, time is the factor that keeps regularity in everyday life (for example, keeping the same starting study time every day). I recommend this approach for most students.

Task-oriented management — Division of time and production is tallied by task. The task must be completed regardless of the time required, in this approach. This approach requires extreme dedication and focus to the task, and although it works for some students, I advise students to use the other approach. Realistically, both approaches are used in everyday life but by consciously choosing one we are able to better manage our time.

U

Update letter — A letter of interest and update sent to colleges when you are on the waitlist to convince an acceptance, usually consisting of any awards, intent to attend if admitted, or notification of contact with school professors or students.

V

Vision pyramid — A schematic showing that academics forms the base of an individual, leading to the ability to develop passion through activities, and eventually reach and develop a vision of who you are and what you see your role in society being.

W

Walk-on — An athlete that makes a varsity team for a particular sport at the collegiate level by trying out once accepted to a school via non-athletic admission. Sometimes borderline athletes are requested to do this method when coaches feel they are not strong enough to be recruited.

The Applicant In Concrete

Terms:

Academic Capability

GPA + SAT/ACT +

SAT Subject Tests

Critical Thinking Ability

Essays +

Recommendations

Personality and Drive

Essays +

Interview

The 10 Common College Admissions Myths

THE FRESHMAN YEAR MYTH

"Freshman year does not matter."

Some upperclassmen or college students may tell you that freshman year does not matter. Let me tell you: IT DOES. Every single year matters because it is time that you *could* be practicing your time management skills, honing your interests, and developing social ties to the community, to friends, and to like-minded students around the world. At the same time, just try your best. Half of the battle is knowing that every year counts. Then you will start working harder because YOU are motivated to work.

THE "BIG THING" MYTH

"You need to do something outside of class so you can write it down on your resume."

This "big thing" could be a competition or award. The myth associated with the "big thing" is that it is an achievement or award. I believe that it can *developed* and can even be your family, it just has to be something you are passionate about.

THE AP TEST MYTH

"Oh, you took all the AP tests, all 17 of them! I took only 16. You are going to be accepted to every college and I am going to be rejected because of that."

I know many parents and some students who believe this myth. Again, this is a FALSE myth. Challenge yourself and take as many AP or IB courses you can. Maybe push yourself further than you think you can handle. The academic preparation you will get is invaluable. At the same time, the difference between 15 or 16 tests is very small and will not be make or break. If your school does not have these exams, do not worry — just do the best you can in your setting.

The availability of AP or IB programs plays a big role. If your school offers many, try to take many but do not worry if you don't take every one. If you school does not offer any, do the best you can in your classes.

THE MYTH OF SENIORITIS

"You got in, and senior year does not matter."

Focus on your schoolwork. Senioritis, laziness and lack of care, does not really exist if you do not let it exist. Your course load during senior year usually is one of the harder academic loads you should be taking and discipline can be shown by consistent grades and strong extracurricular activities. In addition, writing essays takes time and energy and is done during senior year.

THE ONE-TEST WONDER MYTH

"I walked in and got a 2400."

We have all heard the myth about that student who did not take any practice tests, walked in on exam day, and got a 2400. I have never met such an individual. But even if he/she does exist, there are a few reasons why it is possible:

1. He/she thinks EXACTLY like the exam writers (highly unlikely)
2. His/her math skills, writing skills, and reading skills were matched particularly to that exam
3. He/she frankly got lucky

The preparation that the ACT/SAT requires will help you in places other than the SAT. Hard work never goes to waste. It will help you with your college tests and much more, learning how to study. Do not assume that you can walk into the test and ace it.

THE CURVE MYTH

"Take the November SAT, it has an easier curve."

Many students have the opinion that certain months have "steeper curves" for exams, whether it be the ACT, SAT, or the SAT Subject Tests. Although this ends up being statistically true, I think your approach should not be significantly altered by such notions. If you know the method, you will succeed any month. Just focus on learning. I know it is harder said than done, but it will save you paranoia.

Do not believe in these myths. Focus on your own test-taking abilities and your progress. This approach is really the only way to be successful with the exam. You almost have to tunnel yourself into focusing on each exam, each question, and leave the hypothetical grade-grubbing to others. Success will come to those who can succeed at any time.

COMMUNITY SERVICE MYTH

"You need to do community service, colleges like that."

There is a general misconception among parents, students, and some educators that students need to do community service. Sometimes, this idea is extended that the area of community service does not matter — as long as the student does community service this can be "checked off" the necessary checklist of activities.

While I agree that community service is important, I think that you should always do what you love. It could be service for your parents. It could be giving back to your brother. Be sincere with your activities and with yourself. Admissions officers stress community service because it shows that you have a bigger perspective and that you can really think beyond yourself. You can show that in many ways, and that attitude will always come out in your essays. Doing an activity just to have it on the resume is 100 percent counter to this philosophy. Do what you love and show it.

THE TOEFL MYTH

"You must score perfect on the TOEFL!"

Many students applying from international locations to US schools are required to take the TOEFL examination, especially for competitive institutions. The general attitude of perfectionism sometimes carries over to the TOEFL.

The TOEFL's purpose is to credit the ability to converse at university level in the English language, not to discern academic potential or ability. Although a high score would never hurt, perfection is not necessary. Look at the purpose of each exam and consider which the admissions officers would want to know more about: the ability to converse in English or the ability to learn, develop, analyze, and synthesize quickly.

THE PRIVATE COUNSELOR MYTH

"You need a private counselor."

Sometimes some parents and students think that a private counselor is necessary for gaining admission to colleges, especially very competitive institutions. THIS IS NOT TRUE.

Thankfully, with the invention of the Internet and sites like College Discussion, much of the experience and insight that can be gained from a counselor can be scoured by the individual. I will admit I spent thousands of hours on these sites, but if you are not willing to do this then a counselor becomes very valuable.

Still, at the end of the day, the admissions process is an individual process between applicant and admissions officer — not between anyone else. There is no need for a private counselor, but they can be very helpful in finding extracurricular activities particularly.

THE WORK EXPERIENCE MYTH

"It is good for admissions and they will see that you know the value of money! Also, you have little time left; at least you can use your time in this manner!"

While this is right in some regards, it is definitely wrong in others. First, the parent seems to be pushing the idea that work experience must be done to **"resume pad"**, or fill one's resume with activities for the sake of the resume only. This is wrong and one of the common mistakes that parents, students, and counselors make. Do not work for the resume.

At the same time, there are some true elements to the statement above. Working does teach you the value of money and other very good lessons like time management. But often these valuable lessons are mixed with the pragmatics of applying to college and from there a false myth is formed. Be yourself, be honest.

If you are working because you truly are considering a career in a related field or want to work, then work! You are being yourself and genuine. If you are working because you must for financial reasons, then work! You are also being genuine and true. If the second case is yours, be sure to recognize this fact on your application and in your essays.

The Flow of Understanding

Philosophy and Purpose

-What's the point of the application process?
-What are the admissions officers looking for?
-What is my writing style?
-Who am I and how is that shown by what I do?

Tests and Essays

-What are ways to approach the SAT/ACT and the SAT subject tests (tricks, time-saving tactics, other minuta)?

-Which classes do I take to demonstrate my strengths and my potential?

-How do I write essays to convey who I am?

The Interview and Supplementary Materials

-Combine your personalized philosophy and purpose with your concrete exam scores and essays

-By this point, you know who you are, it is easy to convey in the interview and through supplementary materials